Duct Tape and

Dee Dickens

Copyright © 2021 by Dee Dickens

All rights reserved. No part of this publication may be reproduced, distributed, or transmitted in any form or by any means, including photocopying, recording, or other electronic or mechanical methods, without prior written permission of the publisher, except in the case of brief quotations embodied in critical reviews and certain other non-commercial uses permitted by copyright law.

For permission requests, contact the author.

ISBN: 9781723131714

Phil, my love. This is for you, whether you want it or not. Schlaboomf.

Also available from Dee Dickens

I Woke Up Early

An Approximation of Womanhood

The Changeling Child and the Horse

Conversations With the Pixie

Fear of Drowning

Contents

introduction 1

beginnings 8

well, hello stella! 14

bumholes and microwaves 22

hello caller, you're through 28

something, something, darkside 41

a rose by any other name 51

the elephant in the room 57

lazing on a sunny afternoon 67

wait, there's more… 97

knickers 105

the unexpected 117

proposals, indecent and otherwise 126

love, whatever that is 142

here come the girls! 150

the female of the species is more deadly than the male
 154

and now, the end is near 162

acknowledgements 165

about the author 166

introduction

Dear Reader, let me introduce myself. My name is Dee Dickens and as well as being a student, a writer, a poet, mother, and wife, I am a sex worker.

Sex worker. Conjures up an image. Whore, hooker with a heart of gold, street walker, call girl. Fur coats, no knickers, leaning against a wall in a dark and dirty city alley. Madame Cyn, Christine Keeler, the criminally young Jodie Foster in Taxi Driver, Joanna Lumley in Shirley Valentine; whatever springs to your mind, I promise you that the reality is nothing like the telly.

We've all heard the rhetoric round sex work. How no one ever chooses it, that it is only ever because of low economic status. That no little girl ever dreams of being a sex worker, but what can I tell you? As a small child I either wanted to be a sex worker or an opera singer. We listened to an awful lot of opera in my early years, my parents played it to us in our cribs, and I was enthralled, still am, by Maria Callas. She had an incredible voice, incredible coats and incredible presence. I used to parade up and down singing arias and pretending that I was on my way to my yacht post-concert feeling glam and fabulous even in my pining for Aristotle Onassis who had just left me for the frigid American Widow. I had quite the immersive imagination as a child, maybe I was always destined to be a writer. Maria was a diva, The Diva, and as a child who always felt like an ugly duckling, she was something to aspire to. La Divina was not a conventional beauty, she just had something about her. I wanted to be like that.

As for wanting to be a sex worker, I had seen them on childhood Saturday night treat, Kojak and though I didn't know exactly what it involved, they looked exotic and self-sufficient; badass. They were beautiful to me and had someone who really cared about them. Yes, I understand about pimps now and how they are not a Good Thing, but my life has always been held together by duct tape and daddy issues, so I knew no better. Besides, I really liked the shoes. I still really like the shoes. Not that I wear them for work now, it is usually pjs, messy hair, a cat in tow and unbrushed teeth. I'm a real catch.

You have questions, I know. Once they get over the initial shock, everyone does. That initial shock can be funny as hell too. My dad asked if I was making good money. My mother-in-law straight up screamed. She then made me a packed lunch for my train journey home, so I think she still loves me. My sister was just worried about how I pay my taxes. They all wanted to know the same things though. How did I get into it? Why did I get into it? When did I get into it? How do I do it without laughing? Happy to explain. Grab a cuppa, this may take a little while.

It all began in the summer of 2018 when I was turned down for a job at the cheap supermarket, Lidl. Yes, that Lidl. Where the staff seem to be asleep or brain dead most of the time. That Lidl. And they didn't want me. This is a bit embarrassing when you think about it really as I have worked in retail, hospitality, and customer service for 30 plus years, am very intelligent and a hard worker. To be fair to them though, if I had read the responses, I gave to their psychometric bullshit tests, I wouldn't have given me an interview either. I answered honestly, which was a massive mistake as it means that I answered like someone who was used to dealing with a well unionized workplace. Based on some of the questions they asked, I am assuming that Lidl is not a well unionized workplace. I probably scared the crap out of whoever had the thankless task of reading my application. I make no apology for this; I believe that workers are the means of production and that we should be organizing to make our lot better, together. Join a union folks. I have. Oh yes, sex workers have a choice of unions, and I am a proud member.

So, where did that leave me? Broke. Like, proper noodles and ketchup broke. Being a student is difficult enough financially, in the summer it is a killer. You still have rent to pay, you still have to eat, and you are absolutely exhausted physically and mentally. I know that us students have a bad reputation for only getting out of bed to eat noodles and beans, but this could not be further from the truth. Sure, there are those who only fall out of their pits to party or watch Jeremy Kyle but most of them are conscientious, thoughtful, and up to the eyeballs in depression and neuroses. I've just finished my second year and we have had two deaths by suicide on my campus and many, many other attempts. If the government want people to apply to university and get good grades, education should be free. As it isn't then the student loan should be quarterly; and enough to live on. I have opinions on this stuff. If students are going into debt anyway, it might as well be for an amount that would actually keep them alive and able to concentrate on their studies.

But where was I?

I was, broke. I'd written a couple of books but as I was yet a million miles away from the Booker Prize shortlist, I wasn't making anywhere near enough to pay rent and bills etc. I wasn't making enough to buy a coffee to be honest, and though I love that I sold any copies of my other books at all, if I wanted to eat, I would have to make more than £2.26 per month on royalties.

Starving for your art is over romanticized and overrated. I live in an age of internet and Wi-Fi, not freezing garrets and laudanum candles or whatever, and though there was a part of me who thought that dying of consumption Puccini's La Boheme style would have some sort of artistic beauty to it, in reality, I don't even like having a cold; so I did what any self-respecting student who likes eating does, I hit my dad up for some dosh.

Unlike my two sisters, I had never asked my father for anything before. For some reason, probably to do with my autism, I was always proud of the fact that I hadn't but, fuck it, he hadn't had to pay for university for me like he had my brother, that had to be worth something right? I gathered my wits and failing pride around me and skyped him. Wouldn't you know it, the first time I ask him for anything, my usually minted dad didn't have any money to bung my way as he is building a house in Tobago. Because of course he is. Why wouldn't he? Apparently it is for us kids after he is gone. Honestly, I would rather have the cash now, but there you have it. I made a joke to him that I would end up talking to dirty old men on the phone for money and he was outraged. Though, it should be noted, not outraged enough to get his chequebook out, because, you know, house in Tobago. That I will never see, because I am broke. It is his money though, so it is up to him what he does with it.

Hopefully, one day I will make enough of my own to build a house. I doubt it though. Should I ever have that much money, knowing me, I will probably spend it on shoes, coats and a fabulous yacht for pining after a Greek shipping magnate on. Not sure what my husband will think of that, but he knows me well enough to expect it.

As is often the case because of my nature, the more I thought about it though, the more I thought that actually it wouldn't be the worst idea in the world. I wondered how hard it could be. I was good at drama at school, the only reason I didn't end up with an O'Level in it was because I was busy playing Pregnant Teenage Harlot After A Council Flat when I should have been learning soliloquies. This spontaneity is also how I ended up being a ring card girl for the World Kickboxing Championships, drunk skinny dipping in the River Avon in December and riding a horse along Brean Sands in the middle of the night. I'm impulsive and have an overdeveloped sense of fun and adventure. I also have a deep sexy voice and I understand men, the cute simple creatures that they are, so I did some research, chose a persona, created a back story for her and went to work for a phone sex company for the princely sum of 12p per minute.

I have always had an open mind, my sexual tastes are, shall we say, varied; and I have never kink shamed, for who am I to take the piss out of anyone for what floats their boat? However, there are things I have heard, things I have been asked to do, just things, where I earn my money by simply not laughing. Unless it is at the man who likes me to literally guffaw at his penis. That was a good day at work. More of that later.

What I soon realized is that for every type of strange folk out there, there are some sweet ones and some rather scary ones. I realized that every single caller has their own story, and it would be selfish of me to keep them all to myself. Plus, I am broke, and it would really help me out to write a best seller. I have shoes and coats to buy, and out of everything that sells, sex is at the top of the list. So here are the heroes and villains, the sweet and the unsavory in all their unabridged morning glory.

I hope you enjoy them. I have changed the names, just in case, but every word of this has happened. Yes really. Even the stories of Howling Wolf and Microwave Boy.

Grab the lube and butt plugs, get ready, strap yourselves in, it's going to be a bumpy ride.

Dee xxx

beginnings

So how does one get into phone sex work?

One goes online of course. Everything is on the internet these days. Want a jar of pickled eggs? Internet. Want cheese delivered at 3am? Internet. Want to hear a woman tell you yours is the biggest... well, you get the idea. There are various companies in the UK that do this work, though some pay more than others, and some insist on you using a landline rather than a mobile. This was quite impractical for me as I was sharing a house at the time. It is one thing for me to sit and work in the kitchen so no one can hear me, it is quite another to have the phone ringing into the wee hours. I was astounded by the sheer amount of them. I had assumed that in the age of free internet porn the phone sex industry would be on its arse but no. Let's face it, there isn't much you can't see from vanilla missionary to Brazilian fart porn and that costs nothing, so I couldn't understand how the business model of paying to talk to a stranger on the phone could still raise any revenue, but thanks to the wonderful women at Babe Station, the booby jigglers who wave their phones seductively at the camera, and sell you the illusion of actually calling them, I can log on any week night and speak to a plethora of horny men who want to fulfil a fantasy of actually making a woman cum. I have nothing but awe for those women by the way; I am not sure I could be on screen for that long, jiggling and waving without looking thoroughly bored. Fair play to them, in the small hours I sometimes found myself musing on how many did drama at school.

I wondered how hard it could be to do the phone equivalent, at least I wouldn't have to jiggle my boobs, but I had the looking bored bit down pat.

I discovered that there is a process to go through before you start work, you don't just jump on the phone and start oohing and ahhing. You fill in the application, then someone from the office rings you to discuss the job. I suppose it is on the phone so they can check you don't sound like Elmer Fudd, for while I am sure that there is someone out there wanking away at him talking about Shooting Wabbits, that would be quite a niche fetish to have, most people not finding him sexy. Conversation had; they arrange training which you do on the phone. This, to my eternal disappointment, does not mean learning how to talk dirty or fake an orgasm. That would be much fun. Just imagine.

"No Maureen, remember we said 'ooh' then 'ahh' *and then* 'all over my face big boy'. It makes no sense otherwise. Yes, well done Alexandra, that is exactly the wailing we were going for. Joanne,

JOANNE, you'll kill them off if you keep going like that."

To be fair, with talking dirty, you either have it or you don't. I wasn't sure I would, but it turned out I was a natural, and most of us are already more au fait with the sounding more excited than we actually are than we would actually like. I know I am spilling secrets here and I am sure that you think you are all that and a packet of chips, but seriously, do you think that there is a woman in the world who hasn't faked it? Yes, really.

I can hear the hackles raising from here.
"Not *my* woman" I hear you cry.

Yes, your woman too. I *guarantee* you that she has made the appropriate noises just to get you to finish. Or to encourage you to think that you are doing a good job on a day where she can't be arsed and just wants to get on with cooking tea/watching Corrie/reading a book. Or so she can call you a cab without seeming rude (though remind me to tell you about Dean from Swindon and the time I called a taxi for him *during*, interrupting him to ask where he lived; he kept going, bless his heart) and sort herself out properly. And we need to stop that shit you know? Never mind fake moaning, pull him close and whisper 'git gud' in his ear.

Women, if a man is not making rainbows shoot out of your vag while a chorus of unicorns sing and sprinkle glitter over you, tell him. If he matters, he won't mind and will want to do better. If he minds, then he doesn't matter, and you need to find a new one. Seriously. This may be news to some but actually wanting your sexual partner to fulfil you sexually is one of the reasons bras got burned. The bar is low, I get that, but an orgasm, or two, is the *least* you should expect. You're welcome.

What you learn about on the training are the different phone lines that you will be expected to work on and the rules, the dos and don'ts of what you will be expected to talk about.

Firstly, there is clean chat. On this line you can be flirty but not dirty. If they want hardcore chat, then there is an option for that. No under 18's even on this line. It is for chatting about stuff, not muff. I have only ever taken a single call on this line, and he only ended up on it by accident. It was hilarious, I was being clean and telling him about my day, how I took the dog to the vet and went and got my hair and nails done. I could hear his confusion. You see, we're not supposed to tell them they are on the clean line, something about regulations apparently, but eventually his confusion and good manners were overtaken by his horn, and he asked, 'don't you want to hear about my hardon?'. Tells you something about the usual clientele.

Then there is the Australian clean chat, which I thought at first meant I had to pretend to be Australian, and to be honest, I was down with that. I had images of myself breathily telling our Antipodean cousins to throw another shrimp on the barbie, but it wasn't to be. The calls come *in* from Australia, which can be weird at three in the morning when they tell you they are just on their lunch break. Then there is the hardcore line, on which I get most calls, and make up the biggest amount of this book. The dominatrix line is self-explanatory really but the *piece de resistance* is the granny line. I get a *lot* of calls on the granny line. You haven't lived until you have heard a man grunt when you tell him you are 72.

You would think that anything goes in the world of the Phone Actress (yes, that is really my job title, take *that* un-passed drama O'Level) but there are rules.

1. No chatting to anyone you even suspect might be under 18. Even if they give you a correct date of birth on asking, even if they call on a clean chat line (as if), if you think they are underage, you terminate the call.

2. No talking about rape, incest or children. If it isn't legal then we don't talk about it. Plus, eww.

And that is it.

Training is finished, you learn how to log on, how to get onto the system etc and then you get an email from the office congratulating you and telling you it is now time to record your introductions.

well, hello stella!

The recorded messages. These were an absolute joy to do. They are important as they are the thing that might make the difference between a caller choosing to talk to you or not. They are your advert, if you will, a calling card left in a virtual phone box. *Mindy, 22, massage,* for the internet age. It feels like setting up a filthy voicemail message that you hope your dad never hears. Oh, good lord, pray that your dad never hears.

I had to do a recording for each category; clean, dirty, dom, granny. I also had to pick a name. I could have just used my own, it is easy to remember, but when I tried to imagine strangers saying it in a sexy way, I ended up chewing on the bit of vomit that came up into my mouth. So no. I had to pick something else.

Eventually, I decided on the name Stella for my sexy alter ego; it felt right. My mum had a friend with the same name when I was a teenager, and she was my first older woman crush. I was obsessed with the nape of her neck and the way her hair fell out of her ponytail. All I wanted was to caress it. Strange the things you remember isn't it? It sounded like a good name for a sassy older woman, and I figured if I was asked when I was playing young where the name came from I would say that I was named for my great aunt who never married but took lots of lovers of all genders. I also had this image of Marlon Brando every time I thought about a customer shouting my name in the throes of passion and it made me laugh.

I was taking this shit seriously, but not *too* seriously.

Stella is 5'9", long legs, big arse, big tits, blonde (or silver grey on the granny line) curly shoulder length hair, with green eyes and a wicked smile. Hands up, she does look very much like me, ok, pretty much identical, but I figured it would be less to remember when asked. Depending on what line she is on, she is a hotel receptionist or a retired tax advisor who now works part time in a café. When she is Mistress Stella on the dominatrix line, she is scary as fuck and her voice is growly. Like gravel took up smoking to sing jazz. She likes a night out and gets a bit naughty on the prosecco with the girls. She is quite the flirt and likes to get down and dirty on the dance floor. She also really, *really* likes giving blow jobs. Honestly, it is her absolute *favourite* thing to do. (That sound you hear is my eyes rolling all the way back into my head.)

Unsurprisingly, Stella is very popular. Especially with the men who like blow jobs. So Stella is popular with pretty much all men.

Stella has lived quite the life. She has had sex in public, with women, with multiple partners all at the same time. She likes anal, younger men, older men, and she knows exactly how to please them all. Stella is as old as you want her to be, or as young as 18. She is everything to all men and she seems to know instinctively what you will like. There is a reason for that. I hope you are sat down as this might come as a shock. Men are not as complex as they like to think they are. Not when it comes to thinking with the little head instead of the big one.

Shit, men are so bloody easy to read that it almost seems a cheek getting paid if I am honest. Don't think I can't feel the #notallmen indignance coming from you right now. Don't think I can't hear the cries of FEMINAZI echoing across social media. I am not saying that you don't have hopes or dreams or complex emotions, I am saying that as soon as you get a hard on, you can be *anticipated*. So sit down.

Where was I? Oh yes. I wrote out my recorded messages so I would have less of a chance of cracking up laughing and fucking it up, and it worked. At least while I was recording them. Afterwards, I laughed so hard that I had to sit down. An hour later I had the Big Boss ring me up and tell me that the messages I had done were the best she had heard in a long time.

Now, I am a writer, words are my craft, my stock in trade, but I still don't know how I feel about that. I mean, what I wrote was hardly high literature, it was base and obvious and really bloody cheesy to be honest. I can only surmise that either everyone else's were god-awful, or I am an as yet undiscovered titillating porn genius.

You can judge for yourself below. Behold, the Clean, the Hardcore, the Dominatrix and the Granny.

Clean – "Hi guys my name is Stella, and I am a very adventurous and sporty young lady. I love running and going to the gym keep my body in good shape and I take great care over my appearance especially my hair but at the weekend I am a bit of a party animal. I love a glass or two of wine and can get very naughty when I am out on the town with the girls. I get up to all sorts! During the day I work as a receptionist at a hotel, and I get to speak to lots of people. I really love my job to bits as I'm very chatty and I get a real thrill out of meeting people. My friends all say that I am a very caring person, I love animals and I am a great listener. I am really interested in people. Come and chat to me now, so we can get to know each other better. I promise I won't bite! Hope to speak to you soon, take care Stella."

Oh yeah, Stella loves animals and is a good listener. She's a proper upstanding girl. Who gets paid to talk to strangers. Or would if any of them ever wanted to talk to her. I feel a bit sad for clean Stella, she is bored out of her mind, just waiting for a nice boy to call so she can talk to him about cats.

Hardcore – "Hi boys my name is Stella, and I am a very adventurous and totally open-minded woman. I love to keep my body in good shape, and I take great care over my appearance especially with my hair, but at the weekend I cut loose and go wild. I get very naughty when I am out on the town with the girls, and I am very well known for being quite the flirt when I have been drinking wine! I love getting down and dirty on the dance floor, I'm very flexible and I have even had sex with a stranger in the pub garden! I absolutely love sex and my favourite position is doggy as I love to have my hair pulled as I get cock rammed in me, the harder the better. During the day I work as a receptionist at a hotel so as you can imagine I speak to a lot of different people. I really do enjoy my job as I get to see lots of hot people when they come to check in. I have even once fucked a customer in the lobby! I am filthy, aren't I? Speak to me now and I can tell you about it while we wank ourselves off until we come together, I promise you I am a very dirty bitch."

That took a turn for the, well, something, didn't it? She's gone from loving animals to loving cock, which is sort of an animal I suppose. And she loves a bit of doggy. This Stella is very busy indeed. Sorry Clean Stella, it's just the way it is.

Brace yourselves, Mistress Stella is on the way – "Hello all you worthless pussy sluts out there my name is Stella I have very dirty fantasies about making naughty submissive men my sex slaves. I love being controlling and domineering and when I get men in the bedroom they had better do as they are told, or they will feel my displeasure. My best friend is my hand leather whip and if men do not obey my every command, they will feel its bite on them, 10 of the best. I am a striking looking woman and I take care of every part of my body. You had better worship it otherwise I will get very angry and take this out on my pathetic slaves. Speak to me now so I can pleasure my aching pussy, I am here waiting, and you had better not keep me waiting too long or you will receive the sharp end of your Mistresses tongue before I even start my punishments with you."

Yeah, I went there, I said aching pussy. I'm not proud, ok, don't judge me. It is what it is. That being said, what is it about the idea of a pussy aching that men find so fascinating anyway? I know the context is supposed to mean aching for their cock to fill it, but it always sounds a bit medical to me, like what a woman is actually saying is she has some sort of prolapse. Either that or a void of some sort, as that is what I associate with the word aching. It conjures up images of gaping chasms, which, much like a prolapse, is not very sexy. Well, you and I wouldn't think it is sexy, but I am going to tell you about Dave in a bit. Dave would find a prolapse very sexy. More on Dave later, we are about to redeem ourselves somewhat with Granny Stella.

Granny - "Hi I'm Stella a very sexy and older mature lady in my sixties. You know what they say a lady never tells you her real age! (NOTE: I am aware that this makes no sense but go with it) I am retired but a month ago I got a job and I now I work in a local cafe and when I close up in the evening I still don't make it home early as me and my male colleague fuck on the tables while we clean. We are at it like rabbits until I wear him out! I can keep going as long as any man. I love sex and I am a very flirty and dirty older lady and I all I want to do is get a daily fuck, I don't care who from as long as he has a pulse, I want to feel his cock in my cunt. Call me now and listen to granny sliding her fingers into her huge pussy hole, trust me I will make you cum hard and within minutes."

Within minutes. Always appeal to the thrifty. Granny Stella didn't get what she got through wasting money. At least nothing was aching this time. As I said, I was taking this shit seriously.

A few emails and a phone call from the office later I had the go ahead to well, go ahead. So deep breath, log onto the system, the phone rings, I answer and ...

bumholes and microwaves

Enter Jeff. Not his real name but I hope to god that is his real accent. He is from Dorset, (though he pronounced it Dooooorset) you see and has the broadest West Country twang I have ever heard. Ever. And I lived in Bristol for a while.

Jeff was my first and I shall always have a soft spot for him. A hot, wet, soft spot. Good lord the shit I came out with on that first call makes my toes curl. However, the more 'porny' you are, the more they like it. I found out quite early on that key words like, hot, wet, juicy, and throbbing are very popular with your average phone wanking clientele. Jeff certainly liked it, and I am here to tell you, unequivocally, that you haven't lived until you have heard a Dorset man yell "Ooh! Ooh! I just shot my load up your bumhole!" down the phone at you. Ah Jeff, you sweet, sweet man, who wanted nothing more but for me to tell you how good your cock felt in my arse. You had no idea you were my first and I had no idea that I would hear the word Bumhole quite as often as I have since I started this job.

Seriously, what is it with the word bumhole? I get what it is with anal, I am quite the fan of it as it happens, it's filthy and *verboten*, but let's be honest, there are sexier ways to describe it. My tight little arsehole is my favourite, ("Oh yeah, slide that nice juicy cock into my tight little arsehole" etc) shouting bumhole just makes a man sound like a fevered bumpkin, if you'll pardon the pun.

I have heard it in many accents. It has its own charm in all of them. I think Geordie might be my favourite, *bomhwole*, or maybe it was the Essex *bam 'ole*. I have been asked to put things in it, pull things out of it and to run my tongue all around it. I just wish it sounded less, I don't even know how to describe it, it just sounds weird and unsexy. Bumhole. I ask you.

I will admit to being a tad nervous when my first call came through. I utterly blame the patriarchy and its unachievable standards of womanhood for this. Would I be any good at it? Would I be sexy enough? Why did I actually give a shit? (Rent and bills notwithstanding.) My mind raced along with my pulse, doubt entered and for a moment I panicked. *What if I am not sexy enough? What if the men don't get turned on? What if I am shit at this?*

I needn't have worried. What sweet, sweet bumhole Jeff taught me in that first call was that I could be as unsexy as a turnip (though not wishing to cast aspersions on men from Dorset, Jeff might be into that) and the men I spoke to would still find me sexy.

(A very quick note about kinks as there will be a whole chapter dedicated to it, don't you worry. It seems that there is a whole world of kink out there and if you can think of it, there is someone getting their rocks off to it. In my life generally I am the least judgmental person I know, and I have carried this through in my work life. Like to piss yourself while wearing stockings and suspenders, fine. Want to have me blow cigarette smoke in your face, whatever. As long as it isn't to do with your family, children or animals, I'm down. You do you.)

Anyway, back to my first shift. This is where I met Matthew. Lord love him he was a curious one. He sounded quite young so I thought, being the good Phone Sex Operator (PSO) that I am and finding the idea of very young men rather creepy, that I would ask his age. He had been asking me to describe my tongue and said he was soon going to ask me questions about my bottom. That is exactly as he put it too, "I am going to ask you some questions about your bottom." So far, so fifth form. Well, so far so fifth form when I was at school anyway. From what I understand, these days school kids are participating in orgies in the common room and selling crack in the toilets. Well, according to the Daily Mail and its ilk anyway. (Other hateful, sexist, homophobic, racist, transphobic, inaccurate, borderline pedophilic publications are available. Looking at you Metro.) Literally just as I was about to ask him his name, I hear a female voice in the background.

"Alright then love, that's me off now. Don't forget your tea is in the microwave. Four minutes it needs. See you later love."

While this is happening, Matthew has undergone a transformation and has turned into the Harry Enfield character, Kevin. He is grunting away like the disgruntled teenager he clearly is then he comes to the phone and gives me what I am sure he thinks is a cool and suave, "Hi."

It is the closest I have ever come to laughing right at a caller.

"How old are you?". I ask him.
"I don't want to tell you." He replies.
"What's your date of birth?" I counter.
"Can I ask you my questions about your tongue and bottom then tell you?!

No, Matthew, you really can't. Not only am I not allowed to talk to minors, but I also don't actually want to. It is creepy and just not right. Though there is part of me that wonders what kind of question he could ask that couldn't be answered with Big or Round.

Now, I get that there is a whole thing about older women and younger men, I really do. My husband is 15 years younger than me. I know that The Graduate was a thing and that Mrs Robinson is the fantasy of many a young boy. I also know that there are women who get off on it. My friend Brian told me all about how he lost his virginity to an older woman while on his paper round in a Chinese restaurant in Brighton. To be clear, he told us the story in the restaurant, he didn't do his paper round there, that would be odd, he is in his 50's now, I don't think he still has a paper round.

Brian's particular Mrs Robinson taught him the 'ways of the world' apparently. It might have been more useful if she had taught him not to piss himself while he was drunk to be honest.

I promptly hung up on Matthew the Minor. I am sure that when he reaches 18, he will ring back and someone will answer his questions about their tongue and bottom, but it won't be me.

His matter-of-fact curiosity reminds me of the man I think of as Medical Dave. He wanted me to describe my latest smear test to him. He got off on the details and his breathing quickened noticeably when I said the word speculum. You don't even want to know what happened when I said "swept the swab round my cervix" but I am still shuddering.

Fetishes are a strange thing really. From what I understand, they are born in childhood. I have an ex whose mother was one of the horsey set and he has always had a thing for women in jodhpurs, and my own predilections tend towards the young catholic priest and being punished for being a sinner, so I am not judging. Medical Dave might have seen his mother go for a smear when he was young and been affected by it. Sounds reasonable. Not sure what the fuck was going on with Matthew though.

I was starting to get into my stride now. My nerves were gone, and I was starting to enjoy myself. Not in a sexual way, more in an 'Oh my days this is going to make a good book.' type way so I settled in. The rest of the shift was quite mundane really. Mostly men who just wanted to get off, though they come in their own special categories too…

hello caller, you're through

First though, a little bit of background and info on how much I get paid. It used to be that PSOs earned a LOT of money. It used to be £1.50 per minute to call us and life was good. I wish I had jumped on this bandwagon back in the day, as I would have been able to buy my own house with the kind of cash women were making. If you are of a certain age you will remember the adverts for 0891 numbers being all over your telly when you got home from the club. The graphics were loud and the hair big. Life was good. These days, free internet porn has cut into the income of the honest PSO, and they only get charged a paltry 35p per minute. Of that, I get 12p. And believe me, depending on what they want to talk about, a minute can feel like a *very long time*.

There are various kinds of caller I get on an average shift. They range from the cheap to the extravagant.

Enter Mr Cheap As Hell. This guy will have been watching free porn for a while, you will sometimes be able to hear it in the background and will really want to shoot his load (another lovely turn of phrase). He will get himself to the point where he is REALLY VERY CLOSE then ring me. If I am lucky, I will get my name out and the fact that I have big tits before he grunts and hangs up. I get paid *six fucking pence* to hear the guy cum. Christ, if you came up to me in the street and offered me sixpence to listen to you cum, I would tell you to piss off. Loudly. While I am laughing.

I had a guy whose thing was having women look at his cock. He wanted me to download an app so he could send me a picture. Fuck off mate. This isn't Tinder, it is work for me and if you want me to look at your dick you are going to have to pay me a lot more than 12p per minute. I am providing a service and that service needs to be appreciated.

Pay your sex workers more for fuck's sake! If you live near me and ever hear the words 'Cheap motherfucker' being screamed loudly into the dark of the night you now know why. Also, sorry for waking you up.

Next on the list we have Mr Five Minutes. Mr Five Minutes is gentlemanly enough to tell me his name and ask me what I look like. He will then tell me he is naked and horny. Which, let's be honest, isn't much of a surprise. Usually he will have just got out of the shower and will insist on telling me that too, like it will endear him to me because he has made an effort. Mate, this is not a date. I literally could not give a shit where you are, what you look like or the fact that you've given your cock a good wash for me. Dude, you are *supposed* to give your cock a good wash, you know, generally. That being said, Mr Five Minutes, having had a shower, does mean that I get to do my describing a blow job thing. I know I am not going anywhere near it physically, but I am actually more likely to give a phone blow job to a man who says he has just showered. I don't know what that says about me, possibly there is some repressed cheesy nob trauma that I haven't dealt with from my past, who knows?

Many women do not enjoy giving blow jobs. I do not judge those women at all. Patriarchy and the Madonna/Whore dichotomy tells us that Good Girls don't. It's infuriating. The whole 'lady in the streets, whore in the sheets' thing is an impossible standard and totally ignores that women should have the autonomy to do whatever the fuck they like. So, women who like blow jobs feel they can't say so or they are a slag and women who don't are pressured to do it.

It's fucked up and it starts in childhood. I was told as a teenager that a hand job is what you do for your man when you are on your period, so he doesn't stray. Yes, really. Because men will go elsewhere if they don't have sex on tap from you so you must compromise by giving his cock a tug for five days a month. Give me fucking strength.

According to my mother, blow jobs were something that Nice Girls didn't do. Not ever. *DO NOT SWALLOW. YOU WILL GO TO HELL IF YOU SWALLOW HIS DEMON JUICE.* Alright mum, calm your tits.

An old lady once told me that it's called a blow job because if you do get in in your mouth, the first thing you do is blow it out. Fucksake. I laughed so hard and got a valuable lesson in the idea that nobody was born old.

This slut shaming bollocks thinking is pervasive, so imagine the joy in Mr Five Minute's voice when Stella tells him that sucking a nice juicy cock is her favourite thing to do. She bloody loves it and will describe in delicious detail exactly what she is doing, how she is doing it and when.

Full disclosure time, I do actually like it. I got my tongue pierced because I am ridiculously orally fixated and I have to work and sleep sometimes, but when I am on the phone, my love of fellatio serves another purpose. If I am doing the describing, I can control how long he is on the phone, and the longer he takes, the more I get paid for the call. I am learning though to judge from the noises how into it he is getting though. I had one guy go from Mr Five Minutes to Mr Minute and a Half just by Stella telling him she was licking his balls. He did take my pin number though so will be calling me again. He's become a special project for me now and when I can call him Mr Six Minutes I will feel like I have achieved something.

It's the little things, but more about Micro Mark later.

Next up is Half Hour Harry. This guy isn't so worried about the cost, he likes to think that he is Jack the Biscuit, and he doesn't *have* to ring sex lines, he does it because he likes it, and he will tell me all about himself. Let joy abound.

Half Hour Harry is a total bore. The kind of man who had a car phone in the 80's and wears a blue shirt with a white collar, which we know is the devil's attire. Half Hour Harry loves to tell you what he does now. He works in The City, whatever that means, and he drives a zzzzzzzzzz...

I don't actually give a shit about his job, what car he has, where he has been on holiday or what expensive whisky he has in his study, but it takes him time to say it and the longer he is on the phone, yeah, you get the drift. Stella will coo happily and ask him if horsepower actually relates to horses and if he likes the taste of *real* champagne. Half Hour Harry may pay me more but there is something honest about Mr Five Minutes who is just there for the wank. No fucking about with Mr Five Minutes who isn't there to impress me and always says thank you afterwards. Half Hour Harry chats for twenty minutes about himself then expects that will be enough for you to cum. Yeah, this is the big difference, Mr Five Minutes wants to cum, Half Hour Harry is so full of himself that he wants you to. Just by talking to him.

I'll be honest with you, Half Hour Harry, there is only one man who has ever made me cum just by talking to me and it isn't you, no matter what I have led you to believe. Know why it takes me so long, why I say things like "Keep going, that's really turning me on."? It is to keep you on the phone for longer, so I get paid more. Also, when I do finally succumb to your charms, I get to hook you by breathing breathily in a breathy like manner, "That's never happened before, usually I have to pretend to cum. Oh my god." Dear Johnno from Oxford, do you really think you made me cum not once, but three times? I was near the end of my shift, and it meant that I could time it, so I didn't have to take another call afterwards.

Sorry to break it to you hun, every single caller I get tells me he is going to fuck me from behind, you are not the first, not even the first today, but you are going to be the call I end then go and have some toast and play with my cats. Prick.

The last category of actual callers is one I call I Got All Night. You'd think I would love this kind of caller as they are paying more but Christ alive and all the angels, this is where I get the weirdos.

A quick clarification here, I am not kink shaming anyone (there will be a non-judgmental chapter on kinks later in this book). I have said it before and I will say it again, as long as it doesn't involve children, animals, family members or rape I am happy to talk about it on the phone with you. It is not the desires of these men that makes them weird, it is the men themselves.

Back to I Got All Night. These men range in class, though they are generally older. They can be rather repressed or what they consider liberal. I have a feeling that some of them were swingers back in the day. They are the Beatnik Generation, the finest minds, etc, who now read the Guardian, have allotments, drink Fair Trade coffee made from the finest arabica beans and ring women in the middle of the night to cum.

Meet Edward. Edward used to be a voice and acting coach and spoke with a precise yet gravelly received pronunciation. He was 83 years old and warned me he got quite visceral when excited. I braced myself for the inevitable onslaught of testosterone and off we went. Edward and I spent a lovely three quarters of an hour talking about this and that, projection and literature and whose voices I liked that he had coached (Top of the list was Donald Sutherland. Those whisky, honey and cigarette tones are to swoon over. If only he would call, I am sure he would have a thing or two to teach Johnno from Oxford) then we moved onto The Sex. This is what Edward called it.

It happened almost imperceptibly. One moment he was talking about Rodin sculpture and the next he was shouting. Much like Dorset Jeff and his bumhole, you have not heard anything quite like an 83-year-old man yelling "Fuck cunt, fuck cunt, fuck cunt." in perfect RP for ten minutes while he pulls on his cock. It was really something. I just sat there with a confused, yet strangely impressed look on my face till I heard him cum with a scream that made me suspect he had also coached Roger Daltrey on The Who's "Won't Be Fooled Again." He went so quiet afterwards that I was worried I'd killed him, but no, he was just recovering, after which he apologized for being so manly and aggressive.

Bless you Edward. I actually hope we get to chat again. Your phone bill might be massive but so was my grin at introducing you to a sculpture from The Master that you were previously unaware of. I can cope with your sheer sexual energy because you now think of me as a Caryatid, and I like that. It makes a change from being called a dirty girl.

Other notable inductees into this category include the man who I swapped cheese jokes with for an hour who actually made me cry with laughter at how bad his were, Bernie the sheep farmer from Mid Wales who taught me everything I ever needed to know about raddle powder before wanking and saying "Oh dear, oh dear." in a broad North Walian accent every time I said something that excited him.

Turned out that every single thing I said excited him.

It also included the bloke whose thing was breastfeeding and made slurping noises for an hour and ten minutes while I resisted the urge to shout BITTY down the phone at him. I swear most of my 12p per minute is for not laughing my ass off on the phone with these men. It is hard earned some nights. I have a top three in the I Got All Night category, so in reverse order:

Roger. I am so happy that you got to have the time of your life on holiday in Ibiza. I am glad that your ex gave you a threesome with a horny sex worker for your birthday. I very much enjoyed the intimate detail you went into when describing every single element to the night, from the skirt your ex was wearing to the beard the waiter had when you went for dinner. I am grateful to you for following me down every tangent I went on when I said things like 'that sounds hot, tell me more about that.' Thank you for believing that I was actually interested in the shoes you were wearing. Thank you for being gullible enough to believe that your story telling skills were that good that you made me cum three times. Roger, you were a good sport for an hour and a half where I didn't have to talk, and you didn't cum at all. You were nearly the perfect caller but there are two ahead of you. Also, your girlfriend sounds proper hot. Give her my number.

Nick. I proper enjoyed our hour. A self-described 'Schizophrenic with mental issues' you were enormous fun. I don't know whether I enjoyed singing the Pokémon theme tune with you the best or the discussion about whether Godzilla or Boris Johnson would win in a fight more, but it was a wild ride. I still maintain that Godzilla would win because Boris is a fictional character. Thank you for roaring your head off laughing at that. Once I bought into the idea that we were having a conversation on a different plane of existence and went with that, it all made a strange kind of sense and I enjoyed myself immensely.

I am sorry I didn't immediately believe that you were royalty Your Majesty, I should have known from the way you referred to everyone as peasants and promised me my own castle. Thank you for sharing your poetry with me and giving me some excellent feedback on mine. I hope you ring again too because it was really rather lovely to be perceived as a person while I was working. I may not be a Caryatid to you, but you recognized me as a goddess and said your subjects were in dire need of a figurehead to worship. I happily accept my place in your new world.

In first place is the man I am going to call Joe. Joe is my favourite caller ever. Joe spent an hour talking to me about a man who had been flirting with him. Joe had always had girlfriends but had never really met one that he could ever think about settling down with. Joe had a father who beat him if he 'acted like a poof'. Joe was 40 years old and couldn't even say the word gay out loud. Joe was a builder who was worried about coming out at work because he thought the lads might take the piss. Joe cried as he told me that he felt guilty every time he thought about this man who flirted with him. Joe asked me if I thought he might be, you know, that way. I reminded Joe that he had rung a sex line and was talking to me about a man. Joe laughed so long and hard at that I honestly thought he was going to injure himself. I then spent a rather lovely further half an hour with Joe, chatting like we were old friends, planning his outfit and what he was going to say to this guy, giggling like we were on a sleepover. I even went for a pee while we talked, and it didn't faze him. It was the most intimate phone call I had and still have taken, and I am grateful for it. I felt good at the end and could answer the next call with a smile. Joe, I really hope that you went and got your man. Sounds like you deserved him, and he sounded perfect for you. I am happy to have helped at all.

(Yes, I am aware that counselling is cheaper, but I have a far shorter waiting list and am available in the middle of the night.)

So those are my favourites and those are the main categories. There are callers who hang up straight away. A short "Hey, how's it going?" from me and they're off. I know I have a sexy voice, but it isn't a bloody superpower that makes men cum instantly, so I am assuming that nerves got the better of them.

May all of my callers find the nerve to ring me back.

Actually, no, not all of them. There are some men who, if I had my way, would never speak to a woman ever again. Not any woman. Not on the phone and certainly not in real life. It is not often I need to take a break from the calls, but it would be remiss of me to try and paint this job as always fun. Sometimes it is the polar opposite of fun. Buckle up, we're heading to the depths now.

something, something, darkside

Fair warning, this chapter is going to be as dark as shit and you might want to skip it if you think it will upset you. However, if you want to know the reality of working on a phone sex line, not just the funny bits, then take a seat.

I do have fun with some of my callers and most of them are harmless but there have been a few that I hung up on.

Now, hanging up on a caller is very much frowned upon as they will take their business elsewhere if you do it and it is a very competitive industry, but it does happen, and the office are fine with me when I do it as they know full well that there is a good bloody reason.

It isn't because of their specific appetites; it is a sex line after all and not everyone's taste runs to the vanilla. I'm fine with that, my own tastes are as far from vanilla as you can get, but I am all about consent and safety. It shouldn't need saying but if you are going to play then make sure that everyone involved is having a good time.

I get so annoyed when I see things like 'consent is sexy', no it isn't, it's fucking mandatory. If she isn't saying no, it doesn't mean she is automatically saying yes.

If I even get a whiff that someone is not happy or is being coerced or is even considering second thoughts, then I'm done. My vagina dries up like the Serengeti and I switch into protective mode. Though there are some that find that sexy, those who like to be mothered, if this happens then I'm nowhere even close to being in the mood and I will kick the shit out of anyone who tries it at that point.

Like, when I am looking for playmates for myself and hubby, I make sure that both people are into it. If he won't let me talk to her then it is not happening. If she is doing it to make him happy then likewise. No.

It is one of the reasons that I am very glad that I can hang up the phone if the guy starts talking about rape. Lord knows we are already pressured into sex, whether it is him sulking, pleading or giving us the cold shoulder when we're not into it and it needs to end. Honestly.

Women, we need to stop having sex when we are not in the mood. We need to tell him he is an asshole for sulking, and we need to not get pestered into it either. Seriously, too many of us have encounters where we get home and wonder if what happened the night before was actually assault, then not reporting it because if we aren't sure then how the fuck are we going to convince anyone else? We need to be enforcing our boundaries and we need to be supporting each other when we do.

Men, it bears repeating, consent isn't sexy, it is fucking mandatory. Not only does no mean no but only an enthusiastic yes means yes. Also, you cannot say you have consent if she is incapacitated by alcohol or drugs. Neither do you actually have her consent if you have had to talk her into it. Nor do you have it if you sulk when she is not in the mood. Do yourself a favour and take mixed signals as a no. If you do any of those things then you are not the Nice Guy I am certain you think you are, you are a potential rapist and you should not be anywhere near women.

Don't even try coming at me with the Not All Men bullshit. Firstly, it is enough men that it is a problem. Secondly, if your response to a woman telling you about her issues is to distance yourself by getting defensive then you are part of the problem. Thirdly, the men who behave badly need you to condemn them not defend them. Lastly, if you don't recognize yourself in what I am describing then I am quite obviously not talking to you.

I am talking to you, man who told me he was feeling very naughty because his girlfriend was out, and he was sniffing dirty knickers. When I said "Oh, sniffing your girlfriend's dirty panties are you?" he told me, in a tone that suggested that I was the idiot that he was sniffing his mum

and his sister's knickers. I wasn't sure that
I had heard him correctly, so he repeated
it and told me that they smelled really
sexy. I don't know where to start with this.
I felt scared for his mum, his sister, and his
girlfriend to be honest.

End. Call.

I am talking to you man who asked me
what my name was on the granny line and
when I said Stella, asked if you could call
me Lilly. I thought it a nice name and
probably the same as an older woman or
teacher he fancied. No. It was his mother's
name and he thought she was really sexy
and wanted to fuck her. Calm your tits
Oedipus, I'm prepared to pretend to be
your primary school teacher but not the
fucking woman who birthed you. Freud
would have a great time with this one. I
have never found my father sexy, though
most of my mates do, so I just don't get it.

End. Call.

Speaking of school, I am talking to you,
guy who rang and wanted me to dress in

school uniform. Now, I have a strange relationship with this sort of thing. I don't mind doing it in real life with The Husband because he can clearly see that I am not a child, he doesn't want to have sex with a child, he wants to have sex with his wife dressed in school uniform so he can make up for the fact that he didn't get his first kiss till he was 17. (Sorry babe). And it is really hot. When I am on the phone it feels different. Very different. With this man it felt sinister. My hackles were up, and I tried to say I was just leaving sixth form. Which would make me 18.

He growled at me; said I was leaving year six. Which would make me 11. He then said, "I am going to fuck you little girl."

"No, you fucking well are not." I replied.

End. Fucking. Call.

He isn't alone either. There are lots of men who while I am talking to them will ask me questions relating to what I was like as a teenager with the boys. One asked me if I liked to touch myself when I was five. These men make me feel sick. They are finding children sexy. They are paedophiles. I won't have it when they tell me that it is just a fantasy and that they aren't doing it 'for real'. It isn't harmless fun and I am not doing children a favour if I let them explore with me instead. I don't want them to have an 'outlet'. I don't want them to do anything apart from die. Horribly. My non-judgmental streak has no time for your perversion, and I would happily kill you myself. Slowly. And I would smile while I was doing it too.

As dark as that was, it isn't as dark as Alex. Alex didn't do anything that contravened any rules so I could not end the call. He wasn't under 18, he wasn't talking about incest, rape, or children. He didn't want to shag a hamster, but his was the worst call I have had to date, and I had to call the office and take the rest of the day off when it was over. To this day, if a caller introduces himself as Alex, even if it is not *this* Alex, I go cold all over. The very name fills me with dread and sends my fight or flight reflex into overdrive.

You see, Alex likes to be in control. I don't usually mind that, I can be quite the submissive when the mood takes me, but Alex has his way of getting off and he doesn't care if the woman is enjoying it. In fact, Alex gets off on women not enjoying it. That he likes his women submissive is fine by me, but Alex likes his subs to cry. Not just a tear or two, he likes them to sob, loud, gut wrenching sobs. Even that wouldn't be too bad, but he likes his subs to talk while they cry. He likes them to say things like:

"I'm sorry I'm so worthless, I'll do better, I promise."

"I am ugly, and you are right to hate me."

"Please hit me, I am not deserving of your kindness."

All stuff that would not feel so bad if women didn't hear it and fear it all of the fucking time. And if Alex didn't like to call women whores and cunts while he tells them to stuff their underwear into their cunts while biting on their lips hard enough to make them bleed, and cry you bitch, cry harder and louder.

When I cried, he laughed and it was that, that what made it so horrific. He was laughing and wanking as I sobbed.

Was it awful? Yes. It was beyond awful. It brought up memories in me that I had thought long buried and triggered the worst PTSD attack I had experienced in a long while. It took me days to recover. Did I do everything he asked? Yes. There was a part of me that wanted to, and a part of me that couldn't help but acquiesce to what he needed and that was scary as fuck.

My demons did not get where they are now by being predictable, the tricksy little bastards.

Did I end the call? No. It was a 45-minute terror ride and Alex is a dangerous man. A very fucking dangerous man.

Women know when they have had a lucky escape and I got mine by telling him I only worked Saturdays. I never work Saturdays. And because I never want to hear that voice again, I never will.

I think we could all probably do with a stiff drink and a break after that, so honesty achieved, maybe we should talk about something a bit more fun. How about we talk about Stella?

a rose by any other name

There are, in fact, three Stellas; Young Stella, Dominatrix Stella and Granny Stella. Young Stella is whatever age you want her to be, as long as that is 18 or over, between 25 and 28 seems to be popular though. Granny Stella is always 73. Yes, oh eagle eyed one, she started off at 72 in the introduction, but I had a birthday after I started writing this book so the Stellas age with me. Dominatrix Stella is going to get a whole chapter of her own so for now we will just concentrate on the Younger and Older.

Both Stellas were named after a great aunt who was a Right Character, who never married or had children. What Great Aunt Stella did have was lots of lovers of various genders and a very good time, right up to the moment she was killed in a trapeze accident, drunk on vodka, having just shagged most of a circus acrobatic troop at the age of 73. Young Stella idolized her as a child for many reasons, the stories, the rolling eyes that went with them, the tone of voice people used when talking about her, which made her sound like the wildest, most legendary woman in the world. To Young Stella she was Mata Hari and Amelia Ehrhart all rolled into one. Exciting and otherworldly.

Mostly though, Young Stella adored her great aunt because she always bought her the most inappropriate presents.

At her 15th birthday party she arrived half cut and brandishing a vibrator so her young namesake would never have to rely on anyone for pleasure and therefore "wouldn't put up with a shit shag ever". As an adult, Young Stella has never ever put up with a shit shag. Great Aunt Stella would be both proud of her niece and very amused at the conversation the poor girl keeps having to have with her parents about how she doesn't have to act *exactly* like her Aunt.

As we have seen in previous chapters, Young Stella works as a hotel receptionist and likes to fuck customers and get wild on the prosecco. I know, it seems a bit cliched like a bad 'Confessions of a...' film from the 70's. If you are too young to remember them, good for you. You never had to see a horny, scarecrow haired Robin Asquith running around making cockney grunting sounds. You got off light. I didn't want that for my Stella, so I wanted it to feel like there was more to her.

Young Stella is 5'9", 34" inside leg, shoulder length blonde hair, green eyes, a nice round bum and has massive, though natural, 34HH boobs.

Young Stella loves to suck cock and be fucked in the arse. She likes multiple partners all at the same time and has no intention of settling down, she is having far too much fun. I am very fond of Young Stella and am looking forward to finding out what adventures she gets up to. She loves to spin a tale and spends hours telling callers about her antics, challenging them to think less of her for being in control.

If Young Stella were alive in the 40's and 50's she would have been known as a 'Game Girl'. Come to think of it, those words were uttered often about Great Aunt Stella. That and "Lock up your wives lads, Stella is back in town, and she looks bored."

And with good reason. Stella liked a challenge and bored, lonely housewives were her target demographic. Young Stella is much the same. And good on her.

Granny Stella is very much like Great Aunt Stella where it comes to attitude and wildness though she was married to her childhood sweetheart and love of her life, Derek. They had three children, all boys and all grown up with their own families now. Granny Stella loves all six of her grandchildren but after spending 42 years working in tax, she is enjoying having even more fun than she did when her Derek was alive, and lord knows she and her Derek had a *lot* of fun.

Granny Stella, as we have seen, works part time in a café and likes to fuck the waiters. What you didn't know was that Derek used to bring a friend home from the pub sometimes for a threesome and she loved it. She smiles indulgently at the youngsters who think they invented anal, and rimming is something she always did. Granny Stella loves the taste of a man's arsehole. She fucked women while Derek worked away because they didn't consider that cheating and on one memorable wedding anniversary, she brought one home for them both. It was easier than finding something made of tin.

Derek passed away five years ago after a short illness and one of the last things he said to Granny Stella was that she should keep living and enjoying life. Though she was devastated to lose the love of her life, she has followed his advice as an homage to the man he was and the couple they were. Her sons have no idea that their mother is such a wild one, but they do think she spends an inordinate amount of time at yoga classes. Stella says that is where she has been every time they struggle to get hold of her, as it is an easy excuse to remember. It is more likely that she has been dogging with her friend Julia or having a gangbang with four or five younger men. She likes them young, does our Stella, it is the only way they can keep up with her.

Why is it so important to me that the two Stellas have a backstory? Well, though they are similar looking to me, and in a lot of ways have similar sexual appetites, they are not me. I have to have that division between us so that I can do the job. The callers don't speak to me, they speak to a version of Stella. They cannot have me, they cannot fuck me, *I* will not suck their cocks. By making the Stellas so complex I can compartmentalize them and keep myself emotionally safe and separate.

Besides, I'm a writer. I literally cannot stop myself. It's what we do. We build people from the ground up, give them hopes and fears and a history that shaped them. We add bits of people we know, a sprinkling of people we'd like to know and insert some of the braver images of ourselves. This is what I have done with the Stellas. I adore them and won't have them besmirched in any way. They are, both of them, doing their thing without excuse or apology and long may it continue.

One of my customers asked Stella why all women weren't like her, wild and outrageous. Her answer was simple. "Because men don't actually like us like that. It makes us difficult to control." The customer agreed with her and said that unfortunately men were really stupid. Me and all of the Stellas thought he was probably correct there.

As an aside, I'm writing this chapter while on a night shift. It is 2am and it isn't busy. I am exhausted and wondering how I am going to keep myself awake for another four hours. Everyone else is asleep, even the cats. Sometimes, doing this job, I feel very alone. This is when having my Stellas is even more important. They keep me going through the wee hours. Bless their permissive little hearts.

the elephant in the room

I get paid to have sex on the phone with men. I say men, there is nothing stopping women from calling, I would bloody love it if a woman phoned up as it happens, it would be the hottest thing ever, but alas, it has not happened as yet. We are where we are. This means that men wank at me while I talk to them and the inevitability of that is that the orgasm. I think that is why sex is never bad for men. Even if it is mediocre, they still get to orgasm right? He may complain about her technique, her energy, or her refusal to do certain things, but it almost never ends with him having a sneaky tug while she goes to the bathroom, just so the whole thing hasn't been a complete loss.

This is also why sex is not always very good for women. Regardless of what they say about wanting to please women, men don't always make sure they orgasm. I know this is going to come as a shock to some of you, but sometimes it takes us a while, and you wanting to change position every two minutes because you saw it on Pornhub is not helping the situation. Here is a hint fella, if you have to ask if she did, she didn't. Even if she says she did. Off you pop to the bathroom. Take your time. Take your phone. No, no, it's fine. Honestly.

I never need to ask while I'm working though, it

happens right in my ear.

They all sound very different, some more different than others. For your delectation, and because, dammit, if I have to hear it then you have to have an assault on your brain ears too, here are some of the most unusual.

Our first contender for Weirdest Sex Noise is the man I call The Elephant in the Room. He is so named not because he likes to wear knickers when he wanks, but because when he cums, and bless him, he takes an age to do so, (to be fair, he is in his 80's) he sounds like an elephant. A loud, angry elephant that has lost his wife and son to poachers in a badly made cartoon. He literally trumpets his arrival in tones that sound scary, hilarious, and triumphant all at the same time. It is quite the thing. I find myself wanting to check he is ok, ask if he needs an ambulance and sing the opening to The Lion King in equal measure.

Luckily, he only rings once a week or I might finish him off. I do find myself wondering just how much 'man juice', (his words, not mine) he produces while roaring, and I wonder what that says about me. It isn't the splat that I hear sometimes from younger men, which, for some reason known only to them, they think is the sexiest thing in the world. PSA guys, it isn't. When I hear the noise of your 'baby gravy' (again, not my words) hitting your keyboard I am reminded of the sound of seagull shit hitting the promenade. There is nothing sexy about seagull shit. They love it though and get really proud like a puppy that has pooed in the right place and wants to show you.

"Do you hear that baby? That's all for you. Doesn't that sound sexy?"

No. I tell you what does sound sexy though, it's you saying that you have folded the laundry and put it away. Or perhaps that you have cleaned the bathroom. Ooh yeah baby, you scrub that toilet, just how I like it. The sound of an ironing board going up, that's sexy. Nearly as sexy as the words, "I love you and I know that doesn't mean I own you or get to control you." See also, "put your feet up, the kettle's on."

Other notables include the man I call Howling Wolf. Oh yes, it is exactly for the reason you think. Not only does he howl when he cums, but as he gets more excited, he pants and barks. Yes, really. After he finishes, he does this thing that dogs do when they are happy. A kind of snuffle. Makes me want to call him a Good Boy. I absolutely earn my money when he calls because I don't laugh at his whinnying when he is turned on. Howling Wolf calls on three nights a month. Guess which ones? Go on, guess. Yep, the three nights of a full moon. And he calls at least three times a night. I have to listen to Howling Wolf do his thing and not sing 'Werewolves of London' in response nine bloody times. It is a difficult thing I do but if it means a regular caller then who am I to judge him. Next month I might introduce the idea of silver into it and mention the idea of swallowing his Monkshood Sap.

Like I said before, I take this shit seriously.

One of my favourites is The Squeaker. The sound he makes at the moment of climax is an odd one to try to describe, but as I have had to hear it, I should at least try to share the experience with you.

Imagine you are on a Southern Train from Worthing to Barnham at 7.36am (other crap, they should all come back into public ownership train services are available, you may adjust this for your own region) and you are listening to your favourite song on a lovely new pair of headphones. No one has sat next to or opposite you, and you have lots of lovely leg room. It is still early enough that the sun is yet to burn off the light mist over the fields as you trundle on your merry way. There may be a castle in the distance. The morning is idyllic, and your coffee is just starting to take effect. You might be pondering taking an early day and spending some time in a nice pub reading a paper and doing the crossword over a pint and a sarnie. My point is, that though it is early, you are relaxed, and life is good.

Then you hear the tannoy on the train start up and it is faulty. It has a ring to it like feedback and it screeches into your very soul via the pathway of your inner ear. It is loud. So loud it actually hurts you; not in your ears, but in your very existence. Your Zen like calm is shattered and you wince, knowing that you will not get to finish early, that the damp air is going to play havoc with your asthma and that coffee is going right through you but there isn't time to go for a wee before your stop and you are not sure that you will make it to the office. You are now close to the feeling you have when you hear the glass shattering, decibel busting screech of The Squeaker. I should have an alert come up on my phone, so I know to put the ear plugs in really. Didn't think phone sex work would need PPE but there you are.

Drum and Bass combo Chase and Status have an album called No More Idols. On that album is a track called Hypest Hype. In the introduction, a male voice shouts 'CHASE AND STATUS!" after which, another male voice, one who I can only assume is Tempa T says "TEMMMMPPPPPZZZZ!". Go to YouTube and have a listen I will wait. Did you hear him? That sound is exactly the same as the one the RP guy makes in his moment of ecstasy.

There is a bloke called Dave who when he cums, sounds like the ooh in you only get an ooh in Typhoo.

Johnny shouts "Nelson Mandela!"

I have one who sounds like a chimp and one who sounds like he is gargling nails in yoghurt. One who literally sobs in gratitude and one who sounds like a cowboy lassoing a particularly difficult steer, but it occurs to me that I don't actually know what most of them sound like as believe it or not, most of them hang up so I can't hear them. There is something intimate about having an orgasm in front of someone, a vulnerability and that can be quite scary for the poor dears I suppose. It is a shame though; I pride myself on my work ethic and like to know I have done a good job and listening to them cum down the phone at least lets me know that I am indeed sexy enough.

How fucked up is that? I actually give a shit if Steve from Northampton has a good time.

Capitalism has fucked me over good and proper, unlike Steve from Northampton, though I am very good at making them think I have had a good time too.

A few years ago, I was watching some lesbian

porn as I am in the habit of doing, it's hot as fuck and it gets me off very quickly, and there was a woman who actually (I think) had an orgasm in it.

She wasn't screaming, she wasn't yelling, she didn't actually sound like any of the other women I have heard on the many other films I have watched. She sounded small, quiet and *authentic*. It was sexy as hell. I still get a twitch when I think about it. Unfortunately, I lost the link to it when I changed phone, but it has left a lasting impression on me, and it does now on my callers.

When I pretend (and I am definitely pretending, despite what my callers believe) to cum for them, it sounds real. They love it. It is drawn out, so it keeps them on the phone for longer, it is quiet, so it doesn't wake anyone up if I am doing a nightshift and it has a very long deep breathing recovery period. This makes them think it was real and they spend money just to listen to me breathing. If they want to spend money to hear me sound like I have been running, then I am not going to try to stop them. The longer I am on the phone, the fewer callers I have to talk to on my shift, the less likely I am to get Alex and the more money I make. One bloke thinks he made me cum three times in a call. Bless his heart. I had to log off for ten minutes so I could laugh. Three times. I ask you.

This wonderful fake orgasm gets me regular repeat callers too. I just have to say one small sentence.

"Oh my god, that *never* happens! I usually have to pretend to cum."

The suckers lap that shit up. Seriously Steve from Northampton, if you could make a woman cum just by telling her about your shag at a sales conference, you would not need to be ringing me. Ditto the built men who tell me they have ten-inch cocks. Of *course* you do petal, of course you do. I believe you. Honest.

I do like my callers to have a good time but for me, sex work is just work. I don't do it because there is something lacking in me either publicly or privately. There is work and then there is my private life (I'm a freak in the bedroom there too, but that is a whole other book) and ne'er the twain shall meet.

So no, I didn't orgasm. Not even once. Though I will sound just like I did.

In the interest of full disclosure, Young Stella and Granny Stella have similar cum noises. They are both quite understated, but Granny Stella has a touch of vibrato to her oohs. Kind of like when your

Nan is singing Onward Christian Soldiers or something by Roy Orbison.

It is very different in tone and volume to how I actually sound, and I think Great Aunt Stella would approve of that. Especially as she was served with a noise abatement order more than once. More than once she invited the server to join in the noise and merry making. More than once they did. One of them didn't leave for six months and when he did so it was to set up a sex cult in Surrey.

An addendum: I just told one of my callers all about Great Aunt Stella, about the 15th birthday party and how she was a great influence on my life. It became a conversation on how the patriarchy enables slut shaming and that is why he can't find a woman like me in the real world. He got it that women should be able to enjoy sex on their own terms without judgement from anyone. He promised me that he would no longer allow slut shaming to take place in front of him. I feel like I am improving the world view of people who call sex lines, one conversation at a time.

I also introduced him to his own arsehole. He'd never been rimmed before so I got him to lick his finger and stroke his arse so that he could imagine it was me. He really got into it. Honestly, I have never heard anyone groan like that at a wet finger before.

It would seem I liberated James in more ways than one, and Toxic Masculinity cast aside for a glorious moment, I left him three fingers deep and sob cumming.

"Vive La Anal!" and "Give us sexual autonomy or give us death!" May not sound like great slogans, but a revolution is necessary if we are going to end the war against women, and let's face it, who would rather go and oppress people than have a massive prostate based orgasm?

lazing on a sunny afternoon

Thank you for your patience, here is the part of the book you have all been waiting for. The part where I tell you about the weird stuff. Guys, gals, non-binary pals, it is time for kink section! I figure that as I am making up names that the men involved can endure a bit of finger pointing and laughing. So, fasten your seatbelts, put your chairs and trays in an upright position and keep your arms and legs inside the vehicle at all times. It's going to be bumpy ride.

I have learned much about kink since I have been doing this job. I used to think that I was quite kinky, I have some fantasies that people I have told find very strange. For instance, I had a guy dump me on the spot when I told him my ultimate fantasy was to give confession then get fucked by the priest as way of penance. (Has since been done and it was *awesome* by the way). Yet, sexy nun outfits are two a penny. I know. I bought two. If I want him to play doctor, then that is a 'bit weird' but nurses' outfits have kept the porn industry running for millennia. I have three of them. I also have cheerleader and schoolgirl outfits. It would seem that men just have to turn up to be thought of as sexy while women have to make a bloody production out of it.

I think I should address here the cheerleader/schoolgirl thing. I have touched on it before but as long as the person I am with understands that I am never going to pretend to be under 18 its all good. As well as having both those outfits, I also have a Storm/Catwoman one and can generally improvise on what is wanted. It is a fantasy, nothing more, but I won't be part of anything that involves family, children, rape or animals. I am still an autonomous person and I reserve the right not to get you off, even if I am being paid. Paying me does not mean you own me, it means you are renting my time, and even then, I am allowed to decide to evict you from my presence if I like.

So, with that in mind, onto some of the more left field requests I have had.

One of the first kinks I had was the

guy; let's call him Suzy, because, well, I did call him Suzy; who wanted me to dress him up and take him to a salon. This guy just wanted a friend to play dress up with, that is what got him off. I really got into it, and he came while I was sat across him plucking his eyebrows. By that point he had been dressed in some classy underwear and had his hair done tastefully. There is an awful tendency for men who cross dress to do so in underwear that most of us wouldn't go near for the sheer reason that any accidental rubbing of it would cause that much dry friction that it would be a fire hazard. I know that the companies that supply this crap are discreet, but dammit, these men pay a lot of money, and they deserve decent underwear. (Note to self: business idea, get nicer underwear for men.)

It was quite innocent, and I taught him that sexy could be defined as many things. He was truly grateful for the advice and the wank, and I wish him well.

Suzy rang me back not long ago actually; he is having a lovely time buying underwear and has got some amazing stuff.

Makes me happy that he has also been learning about how to do make up better. You do you Suzy! Blend girl, blend!

Next up we have The Oedipals. They're a strange bunch. Meet Danny. Danny has a bit of a thing for his mother-in-law. His fantasy was that she would come around when his wife, Sue, was out. She would have just been shopping and wanting to try on her purchases. Danny would be quite happy to give his opinion on what she had bought if she wanted. She did want. She very much wanted.

Now, I did some research on this, don't want you thinking that it's all made up, and the Mother-in-Law fantasy is really, *really* common. Women, if you have a son in law, odds are he has thought about fucking you. Often. Apparently, there is something about someone like his wife, but with more experience that is really sexy. While I am absolutely certain that my son in law harbours zero sexual fantasies about me, my son's friends have often said I am fuckable so I kind of get it. I have never fancied any of my in laws male or female and I am sure they are very pleased to hear it.

Back to Danny. That his fantasy was that the mother-in-law had bought a PVC catsuit wasn't the strange thing, that she would choose to try it on in his house wasn't the strange thing either. That Sue came home early and caught us fucking and decided to join in wasn't the strangest thing, Danny assured me that she was Sue's step mum not biological mum, so "it's not that weird really."

No, the strangest thing was that we really got into the role play. Like really got into it. When I said I was going to use his room because it had "the big mirror in it" he said he would put the kettle on. "One sugar isn't it?" he asked.

Now, I know intellectually that I had never spoken to Danny before in my life, he wasn't actually my son in law and he had never ever made me a cup of tea, but dammit, I was annoyed that he didn't know I take two sugars and I really told him off about it. In the middle of a roleplay about him fucking his mother-in-law while she wore a PVC catsuit.

I won't lie, at that point I started to ponder the whole nature of my existence. Who was I that a random man on the phone, who at this point was audibly wanking, would piss me off by not knowing that I take two sugars? What did this say about me?

Luckily, I was snapped out of my reverie by Dan telling me that I looked sexy as hell and asking me if I needed a hand undoing the crotch zip which brought me back to earth with a bump.

Dan was so impressed with me that he proposed. I told him that Sue might have objections to that and besides, I couldn't even contemplate marrying someone who didn't know how many sugars I take in my tea.

Other notable Oedipals include the one who said his girlfriend was out and he was sniffing dirty knickers.

"Her dirty knickers?"

"No," he says, in a tone that suggests that I am the weird and idiotic one, "my mum's."

Well, of course. Silly me.

Some of them accuse me of being closed minded when I won't go there with them. They say that they thought my type would be more open to it. I am not sure what they mean by that or how I should take it. I am assuming they mean phone whore when they say my type. I suppose that is what I am. People pay to have phone sex with me and as they can't see me, I can be anything to them, but fuck it, I am a human being and I will not be taking part in incest, real or imagined. So you can kiss my ass mother fuckers.

It worries me how many men want to actually fuck their mums. I wonder how loveless their lives are that they sexually yearn for the women who gave them life. I am sure that Freud had plenty to say about it, and though I hate the idea that he was right about anything, the insufferable prick, from what I understand, if he rang me today, he would be telling me about his mother, if you know what I mean.

Onto the next, less maternal one. Turns out that The Danger Wank is a thing.

Say hello to Terry. Terry is a painter and decorator from Essex. Terry has a routine on the last day of being in a client's house; once everything is done, all the tools put in the van and the hoover run around. It is then that Terry likes to slip off his coveralls, get himself comfy and use the client's phone to call a sex line. He knows he can get caught at any time and that is the thrill for him, and he likes to let you know; to cut it close.

Now, in the sort of house inhabited by the kind of people who can and do employ a painter and decorator, there is likely to be more than one landline telephone.

On the day that he called me, Terry had clearly not factored this in and was quite surprised to hear spluttering on the end of the line. I don't know if he thought it was me to start with, but he was shocked into finishing when he realized it was the owner of the house on the upstairs extension. Though I'd warrant not as surprised as the house owner was to hear me faking an orgasm while Terry fapped for England. I can only assume that the 20 minutes on the phone with me was deducted from his final invoice.

    There are a group of mainly older men who get off on posh sounding women who swear. Luckily for them I generally swear like a navvy with a stubbed toe, so they are very happy. It isn't that I don't have the vocabulary not to, it's that I enjoy it, there is something rather visceral and sexy about saying fuck rather than fudge. Makes me feel real; makes me feel alive. There are men who feel the same way. There was one particular one who sticks in my mind, probably because he was on the line for an hour and ten minutes, and it was some of the easiest money I have made in this job.

    Gerald has a wife called Emma who likes to prick tease him. Emma goes away on conferences quite often and she winds him up about all the cock she is going to tease while she is gone. Gerald fucking loves it.

Gerald took half an hour to explain to me exactly what Emma does. It wasn't that difficult. Basically, she says fuck a lot and chats men up in bars sans bra while Gerald watches. He then asked me what I would do to prick tease him. He asked me, a writer, to tell him how I would tease him. Oh Gerald, you sweet summer child, prepare for your phone bill to go through the roof, one thing I am very good at is building up a story. Forty minutes later he is panting and swearing at me and telling me I am the equal of his wife. Mate, I am ten times better than your wife and you know it. Sorry Emma, it is what it is.

I saw a meme once that said, "I Love Posh Women Who Swear A Lot." And it reminded me of Gerald and Emma. I don't know where the maker of said meme got the idea from, but I have a sneaking suspicion that she has been a PSO at some point.

Learning lots yet? Here is another

lesson for you.

Coprophilia and Urophilia sound a bit like Greek Gods, don't they? Robed and wreathed, sitting on Mount Olympus wondering why Daddy Zeus finds it impossible to keep his dick in his toga. They are, however, the technical names for Scat play and Golden Showers. Yes, my friends, people who sexually enjoy the waste humans produce from ingesting food and drink are out there and they are willing to pay 35p per minute to talk about it.

As Dr Dre might have said, meet Stan. Unlike Suzy, Stan has exquisite taste in underwear and likes to describe what he is wearing in glorious detail. If my kink was imagining lavish and lovingly described underwear I will never be able to afford I would be in seventh heaven. Stan knows his shoes too. He was wearing kid leather 5" stiletto heels with a pointed toe and an ankle strap when I spoke to him. He didn't know it, but Stan was wearing my foot Kryptonite. I have the Primark version of these shoes and I am not ashamed to admit that when I bought them I moved my shoe rack to a position where they would be the last thing I saw on going to sleep and the first thing I saw when I woke up. They are beautiful, glorious shoes and I love them. As a side note, I love pretty shoes and have lots of them that I have never worn. I don't even care. They are my babies and I cherish them. Not in a weird way though. Honest.

I was very interested in what Stan was going to do next. Stan, it turns out, likes to be punished for pissing on his lovely stockings. He pissed everywhere, on the camisole, on the knickers, on the stockings and yes, *on the lovely, lovely shoes*. Punish him? I wanted to bloody kill him! I'm afraid to say I took my grief about the shoes out on poor Stan and made him do all sorts of things, including licking them clean; not just roleplay, I actually made him lick them while I listened; it lessened the hurt slightly, but I was still annoyed. My ultimate punishment for Stan was to make him handwash his delicates, then wank with a washing up sponge. The rough side. And he did it, and he loved it. And now, I am Sisyphus, and my boulder is having to listen to him destroy the shoes twice a week ("I've never come across anyone so imaginative where it comes to punishment before Stella") when Stan calls. It's a hard life, especially for Stan.

The request for pissing is very common though and I have more than once merged a customer kink with my actual need to go for a pee. I started this job during a heatwave, and, as we well know, it is important to stay hydrated. It is quite often that I need to go mid shift. The customer was very happy, I was very relieved, and it was an extra five minutes on the phone.

I have had men ask me to piss in their mouths, on their cocks, in their hair then massage it like shampoo, all over them and on one quite memorable and oddly specific call, all over the kitchen floor so he could skate in it. Yeah, I know. I was a bit worried about that one, it really hadn't been risk assessed. He could slip and bang his head, but I daren't mention a helmet or lord knows where the conversation would end up!

There is also the guy who wanted to be my personal toilet paper. He wanted me to drink tea all day, I am not even making this up, then he wanted me to never wipe because he would lick me clean every time I had a pee. Every. Single. Time. My first thought was "great, now I can't even have a pee in peace!" and my second was "How much tea could I safely consume in a day?" I am scared to Google it just in case my weird brain dares me to better it.

Then there are the shitters. Now, I have heard my arse referred to as my asshole, my bum hole, and my chocolate starfish on the phone, but really, honestly, what kind of man thinks I am going to be turned on by the phrase "I want to lick your shitbox clean."? He wouldn't stop saying it. He had his fingers in my shitbox, his tongue in my shitbox, and his cock in my shitbox. Every single time he said it I was thinking about 80's girl group Fuzzbox, the singer I had a massive crush on, and I spent most of our time together trying to remember what their one hit wonder was. It was most distracting. I looked it up after the call. It was Pink Sunshine, which most certainly does not come out of my shitbox, in case you were wondering.

There was a guy who found constipation sexy. He just wanted me to pretend to try to force a shit out, grunting and groaning while he tossed himself off. I am sure my neighbours now think I have piles or something. I also had to log off afterwards and go and actually have a poo. All that straining I expect.

I don't what it is, maybe I am the weird one, but I just don't find poo sexy. I know plenty of you do and I am honestly not judging, it just isn't my thing. It meant I missed out on shagging a glorious creature called Stacey once because she was really into it, and I wasn't going there. She was dressed as a bunny girl at the time for fuck's sake, like, OMG this woman was insanely hot. Regrets, I have a few, but hot as she was, because she wanted to take a shit on my tits, one of them is not turning down Stacey. Especially after speaking to this next customer.

Enter Scatman. No, not an alternative recording of a Metallica song, but a 25-year-old man who told me he likes to get a bit filthy. "Yeah, right." thinks I, "There is nothing a 25-year-old can teach me in the filthy stakes." There may even have been a pfft noise made. If you could see me now. I am still shaking my head at my own hubris. I was new, I knew no better so I said the ill-fated words, "Bring it on."

You have no idea just how vanilla you are until you have had someone tell you how he is thinking about you sitting on the toilet, still wearing knickers, pissing and shitting in glorious technicolour detail. I felt very fucking vanilla when he asked me to slide the knickers off, put them on him and squish the shit all over his balls while he wanked. God love him, he had heard my challenge and risen to it as it were. He said he would ring me again as he liked me and next time, *next time*, he would get *really* dirty with me. He was just getting started. Good lord. My brain shuddered and my mind can only comprehend one way it *could* get any filthier and just in case, I no longer eat for at least an hour before my shift. Nor will I underestimate 25-year-olds.

There is a kink that is linked to this that I cannot quite get my head around. Logically,

I know that those who enjoy it like the feeling of being helpless and out of control and I am not judging that, when I have spent a day making decisions, I won't even decide what to cook for tea, but emotionally, sexually, it just isn't my thing, and I don't get it.

I am talking, of course, about the Adult Baby. I have only dealt with one of them, Adam, but I am his favourite, and he rings me often. Apparently, I am the first not to laugh at him, I go with his scenarios mainly, and I am really very good at doing different voices. I was having a three-way argument as his mum, her boyfriend, and his auntie Sharon at one point.

Adam likes his mummy to be a bit common, and though I don't want to play into stereotypes about the working classes, he does pay well. He likes that I know how to change a nappy, and that I play despairing young mum so well. Adam love, I was the despairing young mum, I had my first baby at 17 years old at a time when teenage mothers were even more vilified than they are now if you can believe such a thing, so I get it.

Adam likes his scenarios to be full of dirt, poverty and adults shouting and swearing. I am not sure if this is because he did live like that or he didn't, but either way, it floats his boat. Adam in his scenarios has a little sister who is much loved, and we have discovered, only today that his dad is called Mikey. Every time he calls, we are building this fantasy world up, this morning he had Cheesy Wotsits for breakfast, which is how you know it is fantasy. In real life I would go nowhere near them as Cheesy Wotsits are the devil's food, second only to Cheesy Quavers. Before you get thinking I am a cheese hater, I am not. I love the stuff from the plastic like slices through a mature cheddar, all the way to a Danish blue. I just don't like cheesy snacks. They smell like baby puke. Which is ironic I suppose, considering who I am getting to pretend to eat them.

Adam is quite harmless, and we get along well. What I have learned is that there is actually very little nappy changing in the world of the Adult Baby and Mummy, paraphilic infantilism is as complex as it is varied, but when it happens it is shitty as hell.

I have just had a very long chat online to a man called Seb. It was a long negotiation that ultimately failed, even though the money was *very* good.

Seb wanted to pay me £200 per hour to shit in his mouth, watch him eat it and smear it all over himself. He then wanted me to fuck him in the ass with a strap on, then smear me with my own shit and lick it off very slowly.

Gods help me, I considered it.

It would have been £400 per month for two hours work. I mean, fucking hell. I am a student trying to make ends meet, eat, buy books, which is ridiculously expensive when you are doing a literature degree, and pay rent. £400 per month would pretty much cover my rent.

I suppose this is how women end up covered in shit wondering what happened to their lives.

I considered it.

Just let that sink in. I am a grown woman with a husband and children, good friends. I have self-worth, good politics. I am a feminist and an anarchist. Yet still I considered letting Seb pay me to shit in his mouth.

At the end of the day, £400 a month is £400 a month.

There really is no such thing as ethical consumption under capitalism.

Had a long talk with the husband about it and we decided together, for a variety of reasons, that I wouldn't do it. I've actually got quite a weak stomach and would probably throw up. I decided to do phone work rather than escorting because I couldn't be arsed to get dressed. Going to London twice a month would have been a total ball ache. Finally, and most importantly, Gorgeous Husband didn't want me to do anything sexual in real life with anyone else. So that was that. Me and the Gorgeous One have a really good and happy marriage and the key to that is communication. Sorry Seb, you'll have to get someone else to shit on you.

Also, sorry to the man who wanted me to use my knickers as a toilet for five days then send them to him. I am almost certain that there would be hygiene issues for me there and my sexual health is important to me.

A big 'fuck you' to the man who would have paid me to shit into a container then post it to him, except, he doesn't like the taste of it if the woman has been eating avocado. Mate, you can take away my avocado when you prise it out of my cold, dead fingers.

If you know me in real life you know that I am no longer a smoker after nearly dying of an asthma attack set off by pneumonia at a comedy show (what can I say, Bethany Black is *that* funny) a few years back, but I was always aware of Capnolagnia, the more carcinogenic cousin of Coprophilia and Urophilia. I picture her on Mount Olympus with a ciggy hanging out of her mouth. When I was a smoker there were plenty of men and women who found it sexy. There was one who always liked to light my ciggy at the bar for me, and it got him instantly hard. I indulged it, I liked the idea of being a bit Film Noir Heroine, all sultry and prepossessing, but then the smoking ban happened and that was that. There is, I contend, nothing sexy about trying to light a fag in gale force winds, freezing cold while wrapping your coat round yourself at the side of a pub, so I suppose that is where I come in.

I can pretend to smoke no problem. I still remember the rhythms and how to make it sound like the smoke is leaving my lungs and mouth. However, my first caller who was into it also wanted me to be having my head shaved at the same time. I am not sure what it says about me that I didn't even question his request. He went wild when I told him that I actually have an undercut and that I get my head shaved on a regular basis. I had my shaver in the room, so I switched it on and smoked away. He was so happy and grateful that he ended up staying on the phone for a full minute saying so, which would have more than paid for the electricity I used for the shaver.

I have saved the strangest calls for last. I know right? You didn't think it could get much stranger but mate, it really does.

There is a man who I want to refer to as The Doctor, but I fear I will lose my Whovian credentials if I do. He sounded quite old and had the bedside manner of an actual doctor. Except. He wanted to give me a thorough examination for a pain in my thigh. Now, I haven't had umpteen years at medical school, but I don't remember singing that the thigh bone was connected to the boob bone ever. I have quite a good grasp on human anatomy, I have worked in the Health Service, and I promise you, this bloke is a safeguarding issue. He wanted me to be 20 years old and shy and get me completely naked while I questioned whether or not this was standard procedure. It is not, as far as I am aware, standard procedure to suck a doctor's cock during an examination, but it did make me forget about the pain in my thigh.

I hope for everyone's sake that if this

guy actually was a doctor that he a) has retired and b) is living out what he *didn't* do when he was practicing.

And it gets weirder. Picture the scene. It is 4.30am on a Tuesday and I have been taking calls all night. I am very tired and starting to get a bit punchy. I'm not very good at being overtired so am feeling a bit sick and am desperately waiting for 6am. The sky is starting to get light and in an ideal world I would be sitting in the garden with a cup of coffee, listening to the dawn chorus, rather than the monotone of Mr Amjit Kapoor. That is how he introduced himself. Mr Amjit Kapoor, who likes white women with long black hair to tell him how to wank.

My first thought is to wonder what kind of left-over colonial bullshit this is. I know that Britain subjugated India and I am aware that these scars can take many, many generations to scab over, let alone start to heal, but damn if I don't get some sort of weird pseudo white guilt, which is beyond bizarre as I'm not white and I don't have long black hair. My people were stolen to fill the colonies left behind by slaughtered indigenous people too, but he doesn't know that, and it is 4.30am so I decide to have a bit of fun.

Mr Amjit Kapoor wants me to tell him how to wank, Mr Amjit Kapoor will get his wish. On a side note, the amount of times I have already typed Mr Amjit Kapoor is nowhere near the amount of times I *said* Mr Amjit Kapoor on the call. I find that men like it when you repeat their names to them and this one was so long, I am certain that I got another couple of minutes added to the call just by constantly repeating it.

"Slower, Mr Amjit Kapoor. Faster Mr Amjit Kapoor. Does that feel good Mr Amjit Kapoor?"

To which he answered every time in a dull monotone, "It does White Stella."

Firstly, I have never heard a man sound less excited, and it was pissing me off. It would seem, and believe me, no one was more surprised than I was, I have a semblance of professional pride! Secondly, Fucking White Stella! This call was way more fucked up than most I have had, just in terms of anti-colonial politics, and my very tired head decided to go for broke.

    "Get the olive oil Mr Amjit Kapoor".
    "I don't have any."
    "What do you have?"
    "Sunflower oil?"
    "Go and get it Mr Amjit Kapoor, go and get it."

    I made that fucker splash it everywhere and every time I asked him if it felt good and he called me White Stella in his reply, I got more outrageous. I got him to put it up his arse, all over his cock; I got him to rub his balls with it, I even made him drink some. I started to get hungry for chips and the more I told him to do, the more he liked it and the warmer it got, the more I thought about him smelling of sunflower oil and the more I was craving chips. Then he said, "may I cum now White Stella?" and I started singing White Stella to the tune of Brown Sugar by the Rolling Stones in my head. I was slightly hysterical by now and seriously needing a plate of chips, so I said, more loudly, and more shrilly than I intended, "GO FOR

BROKE MR AMJIT KAPOOR!" and he was so surprised he did a squeak, (lord only knows how he managed to make even that sound monotone), then it was all over.

"I need to clean up now White Stella." He said.
"You do you Mr Amjit Kapoor, I'm going to go get chips." I said.

I no longer do night shifts.

Though Mr Amjit Kapoor does still ring from time to time for a top up.

So now we come to the strangest kink I have come across yet. I looked it up after I took this call because I was as confused as a confused thing what was confused as fuck.

Let me introduce you to George. George has a very specific fetish. George is a fan of Macro/Micro. George wanted me to use my shrink ray to shrink him to exactly one centimetre tall. I don't actually have a shrink ray, but I was intrigued, and being a bit of a Star Wars fan, am well placed to do a good *PEW PEW* sound, so stage one complete.

George is one centimetre tall. Or small. Or something. Then George wanted me to shrink my school bully and tread on her while barefoot so that she squished up in between my toes, which was a bit gross but hey, whatever, it's his call, as long as it isn't illegal or involve listening to Ed Sheeran, I'm down.

So, there I am with *name redacted* in between my toes and actually, George may have a point, that felt really good. Not in a sexual way for me, but maybe I would have paid my therapist far less if she had suggested this as a way to rid myself of anger.

George sees my feet are filthy and wants to lick them clean with his tiny tongue. Okay matey, if that is what you want, I can get down with that.

There I am making the appropriate oohing and ahhing noises and it starts to get weird.

"Starts?" I hear you cry, "how can it get any weirder than that?". Oh, my sweet summer children, what George wants me to do while he licks my feet clean is take pictures and humiliate him. He wants everyone to know how small and pathetic he is, he wants all the women in his life to point at him and ridicule him. George wants the world to know he is tiny and is up for licking feet clean no matter what is on them, the more debasing the better. George licked *name redacted*, dog shit and my husband's cum off my feet, all with his tiny tongue so I thought he deserved some recognition.

Luckily for George, when he called the sex line that night, he reached someone with some social media nous. I told him I had put pictures of him on Instagram with #TinyGeorge #HowPatheticIsThis and he got very excited. I told him #TinyGeorge was trending on Twitter, and I could hear his tiny hand moving up and down his tiny cock in tiny motions as his tiny breathing got heavier. I told him that there had been a discussion on Loose Women about him and the breathing got quicker. It was not unlike a mouse whispering.

Then came the piece de resistance.

"Phillip and Holly have invited you onto This Morning to talk about the #TinyGeorge phenomenon."

Job done. And so was Tiny George.

wait, there's more...

I started to write the chapter on kink in those halcyon days when I was not very far into my journey as a phone actress. Consequently, I had no idea really what was headed my way in terms of the good the bad and the kinky. Just as I think I have heard it all, someone else comes along with a strange request and that idea is blown right out of the water.

Now, I am not sure where this kink was born, nor if there is a fancy Latin name for it, but I suspect it came from a dark place. You see, Mark wants to be fucked by an old woman while he sucks old man cock. Not *older* woman and man, but *OLD*. At least in their 80's. He likes to be debased by them and really used. My role was to watch him and stroke his hair while telling him he was a good boy. It was creepy as fuck.

Talking of the elderly though, I had a man who likes to wank in front of women, consensually, I might add, he was very clear about that, and have them enjoy his hardon. That's cool, I suppose, and from what he told me, he does this a lot. He has wanked at friends, colleagues, the woman who owns the local shop and his neighbours. Once a month he goes over the road to make tea and tidy up for one of his neighbours and her two friends. That they are all in their 70's and she used to be the village postmistress doesn't seem to faze him at all. In fact, he rather likes it. In one of those lovely calls that happens from time to time, he regaled me with stories about them while I relaxed and laughed. He had helicoptered it while they cheered, run the hoover round while they pinched his bottom, and in one strange parody of a glory hole, albeit one run by the Women's Institute, he put his cock through the serving hatch in the kitchen while they played with it. Bless him, he is providing a service, though lord knows what they would say about it at the post office.

Sometimes men can be a bit cagey when it comes to what they want me to do on the phone. I say, "what are you into?" then listen to them as they uhm and ahh, and you can almost hear the shuffling feet. Usually, this means they are into something nefarious, and my guard goes up while my hanging up finger gets ready. Not this time though.

"I have a bit of a strange fetish..."
"Lay it on me, I am sure I will have heard of it."
"I don't think you will have..."
"Well, if I haven't, as long as it doesn't involve rape, being underage, incest or animals, I'll probably be ok with it."
"I'm not sure you will..."
"I promise I won't laugh, Honestly."
"I get turned on by women who burp. Can you burp? Would you burp for me?"

Would I burp for him? Damn right I would! I am one of those people who is able to burp on demand. Not just little burps, but big, rolling, thunderous ones.

I gave him a demo. He liked it. Very much.

Have you ever burped down a

telephone while the man on the other end faps himself into oblivion? No, I hadn't either. It must have been quite a rarity for him too because he had me do it for ten minutes. One of my housemates came upstairs to see if I was ok. I was fine, I was just trying not to laugh at the man who was now growling with pleasure as I belched like the timpani in the 1812 Overture. One handed, I mimed that I was burping for a customer while he tugged away and said housemate was good enough to wait until he got downstairs to roar laughing.

Eventually, The Burpinator came to a messy end. He was most grateful and while I usually have a soft spot for a happy customer, I also had a diaphragm in spasm. It is a real shame that my next customer didn't have a thing for hiccups, which is a fetish, gods help my Google search history, because I had them for the next twenty minutes. The caller didn't seem to mind, just asked me if I would like something to drink. Yeah, water thanks. I don't think sperm is a cure. Though there is probably a fetish for that too.

Though there doesn't seem to be a fancy Latin name for fetishizing working class women, it seems to be very common. Or, as one of my callers put it, "I like fucking scuzzy chav girls. Are you from a council estate? Are you really fucking dirty? Would you suck my cock for a pack of fags to last you till your next Giro?"

Apart from the fact that these assholes are way behind the times; there is no Giro now, everything gets paid into a bank or Post Office account; the sheer classism makes me feel violent. Mr Plum In the Mouth who pronounces it Chaarv, fuck off. I will not be playing into this bullshit where you lord your privileged economic status over us peasants. My money is earned honestly, and Mr Silver Spoon can go and shove his outdated, and quite frankly obscene ideas up his arse.

The last one who tried this on may not have valued my lecture on the disgustingness of objectifying those of lower socio-economic stature but bless him he stayed on the line another two minutes to hear it.

Ever heard anyone drawl at you, voice saturated with lust, smoky like cigars and whiskey in a jazz club? You may well have. I am sure that this kind of voice is, while not common, not exactly sparse. Ever heard them say "I want to lick your sweaty toes."? I have, I wouldn't recommend it. You find yourself saying things like 'Yeah baby, chew that toe jam." It is never your proudest moment.

Gawd bless them though, the foot fetishists, they are easy to please. I had a caller who wanted me to paint my toenails for him while he was on the phone. I got him to pick a colour, and obviously I had to remove the remnants of the old colour and let that evaporate before I got to painting. On the phone. No, I couldn't quite believe it either, but there I was, phone on speaker while I painted my toenails and he listened to me say things like "that's the first coat on, I bet you wish you were here to blow my little piggies dry." Again, not my proudest moment, but a woman gotta eat.

There is a 22-year-old I talk to who likes ankle socks. He is such a sweetheart that I actually put them on so he can hear me take them off. I know that he can't really hear it but bless him, it gets him going to think he can and who am I to disavow him of the notion, especially when he gets me to do it repeatedly at 12p per minute.

Oh, I have to tell you what happened the other day while I think about it. I was recovering from a nasty cold and my voice was broken, like, completely shot. Well, I must have sounded like I had been bitten by a radioactive porn star because suddenly I was like Jessica Rabbit on ketamine, I was Super Porn Woman, and they could not get enough of me. A bloke called Gary rang twice in half an hour, and three times on that shift. Three others instantly reloaded. It was bizarre, especially as one of them was Wanking Frank, and he never usually needs more encouragement than "KEEP WANKING FRANK!" (bless his deaf little heart on a phone line). It was the quickest shift ever and I was more relaxed than I had been while on the phone for ages.

So, here is to you and your weird kinks and fetishes, you keep me going in the dark times and you are hurting no one. Also thank you to Ass_Sniffer from Pantydeal for explaining to me that belch and fart fetishes are borne of the same wind.

Oh, I haven't told you about Pantydeal have I? That is very remiss of me. Get yourself comfy while I grab some throat sweets because this shit is some whole other level.

knickers

I should mention my side project. It came to me in a flash when talking to an elderly man who said he wished he could buy my knickers. He was lonely and it had been years since he'd got the scent of a woman in his nose. It got me wondering why someone like him couldn't. I mean, I have bloody loads of them. Years ago, the woman I refer to as The Wife came round when I split up with the man I refer to as My Late Ex Husband (soon hopefully) and decided that all my knickers were sub-par and I needed to go shopping for new ones. To underline her point, she threw away everything that was old, stained, baggy or had the well-worn elastic looking like "Weird white pubes." Quite a way with words has The Wife.

Who is she, this woman I call The Wife? I met her a long time ago while she was naked. She is often naked. About half an hour after meeting her, I was sat on the loo painting my nails while she and the mutual friend who introduced us, also known as The Wife, had a bath. We all did everything together, ate, slept, took poos while the other showered, even changed tampons in front of each other, we were as close as close could be, but we weren't having sex, so it was like we were married. Hence, we call each other The Wife.

The Wife has a credo where it comes to clothes, and it is startingly simple. If it doesn't make you feel fantastic, don't wear it. She is the William Morris of knickers. So, she got rid of all my rubbish ones and made me go shopping for nice ones. It became a habit and before I knew it, I had so many pairs that I never got to wear any long enough to warrant throwing them out.

The plus side of this is that I now have loads to choose from for my little dirty enterprise.

After talking to the customer who really wished he could sniff my knickers I did a little research into how I would go about selling them. I joined a website, set up a profile, put an ad in their shop and waited.

BAM! Nothing. I'm still waiting for

my first sale from that website and if I have not had any in a month's time, I shall be cancelling my subscription. (UPDATE: I have now sold loads and am more than happy.)

Does this mean I haven't sold any? No, no it does not. What it means is that I have sold them elsewhere. Namely eBay. I am not even kidding. As fast as I put them up, they get bought. (UPDATE: eBay shut me down for breaking their family friendly policy. On a site where I can buy anal beads. Sheesh!) Turns out that a tenner for a pair of knickers I have worn all day is a great price and they are lapping them up. Possibly literally.

I say a tenner, prices vary depending on how long I have worn them, what I have done in them; gym, had sex, not wiped, not showered, the list is endless, and it means more buck for my bang. I am currently in negotiation for a two-week wear on an old lacy thong I have. If it goes through it is worth £250 to me and that is the holding deposit for a house I am looking at in the Rhondda.

I also do custom videos. I have rubbed moisturizer in my boobs, had a wee through knickers and close up, done all sorts of sexual things and in one episode that made me doubt my own sanity, but also paid for a new toaster, filmed myself having a poo. Then wiping, then watching the contents as I flushed. It was really something. A stinky, messy something.

Now I have made you lose the last thing you ate I will tell you about the weird things that get me sales.

That I am a sex worker. Me and you know that I don't get turned on in the slightest but dammit, like Fox Mulder, they want to believe. They want to think that I am lounging around in my underwear being so turned on by my callers that I am sopping wet for them. Seriously, "are you wet?" is the most asked question after "What are you wearing?". First time I heard *that* question asked I was like, seriously, what a fucking cliché. Now I have heard it a hundred times or more I am of the opinion that men have either very little imagination or that they really do want to know what I am wearing.

I once answered the what are you wearing question with "the weight of the capitalist, heteronormative patriarchy." which led to a twenty-minute conversation on how I balance sex work with my feminist beliefs. Quite easily is the answer to that one by the way, I believe that sex work is work and that workers need to be supported. If you have an objection to what I do on moral grounds, by the way, then you don't understand the nature of employment. You sell your body too, I'm just more honest about it. Also, fuck you. I'm in sales and what I am selling is a fantasy that I find them unbearably sexy. I make them believe that their voices alone are enough to make me wet between the legs and squirt enough to need a towel. I'm not even joking. They buy into it too.

They tell me all sorts about themselves that I have to pretend to believe as part of the fantasy. I know that they are old and fat and bald and so do they, but that it not what they are calling for. So I am pleasant with them and tell them I find them gorgeous because "yeah mate, if you are that sexy that women need a towel after being told about your six pack and your 10" cock, I have a question for you. Why the fuck are you ringing me?" wouldn't go down too well.

Which leads me onto dick pics. When I am on Pantydeal negotiating the price for knickers, I get men sending me pictures of their erect penises. It happens all the bloody time. It is irritating as hell for a few reasons. One, I didn't request it. An unsolicited dick pic is still an unsolicited dick pic even if you are sending it to a sex worker. It shows a distinct lack of manners.

Two, I cannot get over the sheer arrogance of men who think that either their pics will get me turned on or that I give a fuck as to whether or not they fancy me. I know they do, or they wouldn't be negotiating with me for the garments that enclose my sacred cave (one of them actually called it that, I nearly puked) and I have a real cock in my life that I enjoy on the regular thanks, and it is far more impressive than the strange looking things that I get sent photos of.

Three, rating penises is a service that is offered. Don't be trying to get freebies you cheap bastards.

I find no conflict between my feminist beliefs and my sex work. My anarchist communist beliefs maybe, but we've already covered that there is no ethical consumption under capitalism. If these idiots think that they are turning me on and want to pay 35p for the pleasure, then more fool them. They always leave educated. I give them permission to be themselves, away from any ideas of toxic masculinity, I give them the space to talk about their fantasies without judgement.

I tell them it is ok to be themselves. I just had a bloke on the phone called David (I'm writing this book between calls) who licks his own spunk "but not in a gay way." I have listened to him and talked to him, and he is going to try sucking a man's cock because 63 years is too long to be in the fucking closet. I talk to them about how it is ok to be gay or bisexual. I tell them that I find a man who is comfortable in his own skin really sexy, and it is true, I do. Just not them.

I spent a lot of hours talking to Ronny who is toilet trade when his girlfriend is away. Ronny worries me as he seems to have little regard not only for his own sexual health, but that of his girlfriend. He kneels down in gay bar toilets sucking any cock that is presented to him before bending over in the stalls and taking any dick that wants him. Bareback too. Though Ronny assures me that he is Absolutely Not Gay. That he brought home ten men and had a coke fueled orgy with them last time his girlfriend went to visit her mother means nothing. Totally no homo.

I talked to Mike who fucks other men when he is away at conferences, he's definitely not gay, he just likes the taste of cock and nobody in his town would understand. Mike goes to conferences that he doesn't actually have to attend so he can do it too. He certainly isn't one of those homosexuals though.

Nor is Nicholas who 'accidentally' ended up fucking his best mate while wearing his wife's thong. I never got to the bottom of how this happened by accident, either the thong wearing or the sex as he didn't go into detail. He told me that they just had hangover horn is all, who of us haven't, and that this has happened many times before means nothing. Of course he isn't gay, or he wouldn't have married a woman. One that he hadn't fucked for six months by his own admission.

It breaks my fucking heart to see the patriarchy reduce these men so much that they ring a sex line to speak to a woman about fucking men in an attempt to keep the longing for cock away. These calls end up more like counselling sessions where I tell them that being their authentic selves is important and will bring them peace. David has been denying who he is for 63 years for fuck's sake, it is about time that we fucked toxic masculinity all the way off and just got the fuck over the idea that men have to be manly. I tell you; I have had anal sex with some big cocks. Any man who takes it up the arse is not a little bitch; he is a fucking warrior.

So yeah, there is no conflict between my feminism and my sex work. I do a good job and provide a service and I do so without embarrassment because fuck it, I am doing some good in the world.

But what about the ones who just ring to get off? It is an honest transaction. I get paid, they get off. I get to eat, and they get to have a connection if only for a moment. You might see it as sordid, I see it as no different to serving fries in McDonalds. It is a service I provide, and I take no shame in it.

There is much talk about sex workers in feminist circles and there are too many people who don't get that any time you go to work doing anything you are selling your labour and that sex workers don't need you to bloody well rescue them. It's so fucking patronizing. If you want to 'help' sex workers, then ring them up and have a nice chat about the weather for an hour. Or hire them for the evening and take them for dinner and to see a film they haven't got around to seeing yet. Or just give them some money if the idea of a woman selling her sexual labour bothers you more than a woman being a cleaner and selling her physical labour. To me there is literally no difference. Take your prudery masquerading as concern for my wellbeing and shove it right up your bumhole.

Where was I? I think I was talking about knickers. Ah yes, that I was. Going to have to go back and re read what I wrote to see where I was up to. Hold on.

Ah yes, that I am a sex worker adds value to the knickers I sell. If I say I have worn them on a shift, then they get far more interest. It is very odd what will sell them. Did you know that couples cum is a thing? Top money for those. Also, skidmarks. Yes skidmarks. The skiddier the better it would seem. Period stains are a really good seller too. I would throw away knickers rather than wash and wear what I have slipped into those zip lock bags.

Men are paying me to go about my business and tell them what I have done. For instance, I tell them when I have been on a three-mile walk. Ironically, that is to the post office to send off the previous stock to their new owners.

The women who work in the village post office love me. They think I am hilarious, and it makes their day when I come in. The first time they asked me what was in the parcel I was selling I whispered it and watched them blush from head to foot. Today they started to ask me questions about how I do it. I shall have a business empire before long.

My customers love a strong scent whether it be cum, piss or sweat. What they don't know is that to keep up with demand I sometimes get my husband to wipe himself down with a pair when he comes back from a run. So, don't tell them yeah? It can be our secret.

the unexpected

      I sometimes get some very lovely calls. It is usually after I have a had a run of calls that make me wonder if I am ready to hang up my mobile and be less sexy for the masses. It will usually follow a call where the bloke has wanted to rape me or have my daughter watch and I am feeling really sick. Those calls can be rough and when they come at the beginning of a shift it is hard to see how you will make it through the rest of it.

      Full disclosure on my mental health incoming: I have depression, anxiety, and complex post-traumatic stress disorder so it can be doubly difficult for me to get through a shift if I have been upset at the beginning of it.

      I know, it's a bit of a cliché isn't it? Abused and depressed woman as sex worker is a trope we are all used to, and this is what in part makes people think that we need rescuing. I don't speak for everyone, but I don't need to be rescued. I am not bloody Rapunzel, nor do I need to be kissed into waking like Snow White and Sleeping Beauty. While I think about it, how weird and creepy is kissing sleeping women and expecting them to fall in love with you? Worse, in the original, she has children while she sleeps. Let that sink in for a moment. Ugh. No ta.

I don't need you to rescue me after a difficult call, I need to take a break and make a cuppa. And I need the lovely calls.

Like the guy I spoke to about Autism. He had told me he was from Leeds. I had said that Leeds was lovely, and he spent the next hour telling me all about his life and how Leeds was a shithole full of crackheads and he hated it. He was hilarious, he had an autistic's comedy timing and he kept me laughing the whole time. I had not long got off the phone with Awful Alex and needed to hear about how the bloke who played Chris Tate in Emmerdale lived up the road from his dad and was a colossal twat. I needed to laugh at the tales he told me from his cricket club. I needed to feel normal for a while, to not feel like I was just a pair of tits and a cunt. We did talk about sex for about half of the call, but in a funny, mates having a laugh way. It was brilliant and I really hope he calls again.

There was a man who I spoke to early on who wanted to tell me all about this man who was flirting with him. He was older and had grey hair and a nice smile under a silver beard and ice blue eyes. He sounded like a total fox and had my caller all of a dither.

My caller had been with women all of his life. He had met this man when he was with his last girlfriend, and she had noticed that there was chemistry between them. It wasn't why they had broken up, but she did tell him, as they parted, that life was too short not to go for what he actually wanted. She sounded like a great woman.

My caller said he had always known that this man was 'that way' and it didn't bother him. We chatted for an hour about how this man was beautiful and elegant and educated and how the light caught his hair and how he melted every time those ice blue eyes met his.

It was wonderful.

At one point my caller asked, "Do you think that I might be, you know, that way?"

"Well you called a sex line to talk to me and have talked about a man you fancy the whole time. What do you think?"

He laughed and laughed, and it felt like it was the first time he had ever given himself permission not to be afraid of the idea.

My caller was a builder on a very macho site. He was worried about what would happen to him if he came out at work. He didn't want to make anyone uncomfortable. I pointed out that as at least one in four people identified as LGBT he could be bloody sure that he wasn't the only one who was 'that way' in his workplace and that his comfort was just as important.

"But what will happen to me in the

future?" he sounded like a man accepting a strange fate.

"You might end up with a boyfriend."

I heard the light enter his eyes. I could hear the possibilities running through his mind, the cogs turning, the penny dropping. I heard the tears.

"I have never thought about it like that. I might have a boyfriend. I am so excited by the thought!"

We spent some time talking about where he would meet him, what he would wear.

"But what should I say?"

"How about hello?"

"I might be really cheeky and say hello darling!"

I was laughing, he was laughing, it was a joyous thing. 3am on a Tuesday morning and I am laughing and discussing shoe choices with a man who is just coming to terms with who he is. I wanted that call to last all night. I went to class the next day with a spring in my step even though I had only had three hours sleep.

I hope he and the silver fox are together now. I hope they are happy, and I hope my caller goes to sleep every night knowing that there is nothing wrong with him and that he deserves to be happy.

I also hope he wore the brown shoes.

Sometimes I have callers who want to watch porn with me. I don't mind it. Generally, it is run of the mill stuff and my search history can take it. I am not going to go on any watch lists by searching 'Rita has her first blow bang." That video is hot as fuck by the way. Rita is my new favourite.

What I didn't expect to see in my Google Search after a shift were things like:
Will my cock actually fall off if I keep playing with it?
Does masturbation actually make you go blind?

Can autistic people have babies?
Does god still love me?

Oh sweet holy fuck was I angry with the people around this caller.

There is a tendency to see disabled people as sexless and it infuriates me. It is somehow distasteful to society that 'defective' people might want to have sex; will nobody think of the children?! Terms like 'breeders' abound like all disabled people are animals. People talk about sterilizing them for their own good, making sure they can't spread their imperfections further. They say that disabled people shouldn't have children because they wouldn't be able to look after them properly.

They deny people access to their own sexuality, they tell them that they will cause themselves damage if they masturbate, that god is watching them, that they will go blind. This is people that disabled people *trust* saying this to them so of course they believe them. They are treated as sexless and yet they are human beings with wants and needs. I could cry with anger when a lovely guy like Richard rings me and makes me google stuff before he will believe that he isn't evil because he masturbates. This poor soul actually thought that his cock would fall off if he kept playing with it. Why? Because his parents and his pastor told him and who could he trust if not them.

Richard, I hope you are having the wank of your life. And I hope that you find the nerve to talk to the girl at the centre that you like. I hope you have lots of lovely consensual sex and if you want to, I hope you have beautiful babies together.

To Richard's parents, fuck you and your outdated views.

After I had calmed Richard down about the imagined impending cock removal doom, we had a lovely conversation about his special interests. He loves planes and it was amazing to hear his voice go from fear to love in the time it took to tell me his favourites.

I now know two autistic people for who the Airbus A380 is everything to them aviation wise and that I could say "Oh yes, I know, the double decker one" made this guy just as happy as if I had said that I had just shoved a dildo up my arse.

Being autistic myself, I got it.

Good luck to you Richard, I hope I helped.

proposals, indecent and otherwise

I'm going to lay this out here. I am good at my job. Really good. If you ring up and get Stella, you had better believe that she is going to give you a good time. Stella has the gift of making you feel like the only man on the planet, and she makes you believe that she is the perfect woman for you. It's quite the knack.

Who am I kidding? It is a piece of piss. These men are so easy to read that I could go on the tarot line to be honest. Tell me your girlfriend is gorgeous and I will offer to fuck her in front of you. Tell me that you like blow jobs and I will spend ten minutes describing one while I browse Amazon for swimsuits. Tell me your thing is giving women pleasure and I will moan my head off. If you are an older man, you will hear my speech about how they are far better as younger men just think they have to show up with a penis. If you are a younger man you will hear how I like them more because they have more energy and are willing to learn.

"Oh no, I don't really like massive cocks, men who have them think that all they have to do is fuck you with them, they have no finesse. I *much* prefer something between six and nine inches."

If you make a happy noise while Stella licks your asshole you had better believe that by the end of the call she will be making you her bitch with a strap on.

It is all about picking up cues and running with them. Constantly adjusting the fantasy according to the sounds you are making and the key words you use. Say I have a sexy British accent and I will go double jolly hockey sticks for you. Call me young lady in the first minute and Stella is 22 years old. Say you like a real woman, and she is 35.

I hate to break it to you boys, but you are not as complex as you think. Especially when all the blood has rushed south. You have one track minds and they are dirt tracks a mile wide. Stella is the one who follows it and makes you think that you are the first to suggest whatever kink it is that you think makes you unique. Really, you're not. You won't even be the first today to suggest putting a finger in my arse.

There is a drawback to being Every Perfect Woman though. Sometimes, just sometimes, they think they are having a relationship with you.

Take Bernie the sheep farmer. No, really, someone take him! He doesn't live that far from me, and he takes his sheep to my local farmers' market. We spent a lovely 20 minutes on the phone because, and I quote, "It isn't very often I get a woman on here who can unnerstan moi acccccent."

Oh Bernie, just because I didn't spend the whole call going *WHAT?* does not mean that I want to meet you at the market for a date. No, it isn't because of your accent, nor is it because of the sheep. It is because talking to you is literally my job and I don't mix business and the inevitable pleasure I am sure it would be to hang out with you and the sheep on top of your mountain.

I think I offended him as he has never rung me back.

Rory from Oxford, you were a really good laugh, and I didn't detest my time on the phone with you. You had some really interesting political ideas, some of which I even managed to change; a bit more reading and I shall have you on a demo representing for black bloc. I know you have a yacht and a big barn conversion Rory, but remember the part where I said that I wasn't overly interested in material possessions past the point of comfort? That means that we are not meant to be, I don't want you to drive down here and whisk me away somewhere exotic. Just because I laughed at your jokes does not mean that we are fated. I mean, for fuck's sake Rory, if that is all it takes to win your heart then I worry for your self-esteem. Oh wait, you have a sports car, a massive barn conversion and a yacht. I think we have a glimpse into your self-esteem there. As you were mate.

Dan with the mother-in-law fantasy.

You were fun. I mean it, we had a blast and even though you didn't remember how many sugars I had in my tea (still annoyed about that by the way) you seemed like a half decent sort. I mean, apart from the wanting to roger your mother-in-law senseless, though I am not going to judge you on that really, I have found it is quite common. There are a few reasons that I turned down your very sweet marriage proposal.

1) I am in fact already married to a wonderful man who knows me and loves me for who I am. He respects me and cherishes me and advocates for me and encourages me. He is my world, and you could never ever measure up. He also knows how many sugars I take in my tea.
2) You already have a wife. Sue sounds lovely to be honest and I would totally fuck her but live with you both in your house where we are both your wives? No ta Dan. The patriarchy already expects too much of women, so I have no wish to be your concubine or second wife.

Besides, I am not entirely sure that you have run this past Sue.
3) Pretending to be your latex and PVC loving mother-in-law was fun, but it was work. I really hope you ring again as it was a lovely diversion from everyone who just wanted to cum in my arse that day.
4) You didn't remember how many sugars I took in my tea.
5)

Don't take it personally, you wouldn't like being married to me and my mum looks like Skeletor so you wouldn't be able to fantasize about her. Unless you are *really* into He-Man. Again, I am not judging.

Remember the guy I swapped cheese jokes with? He had rung up really horny, I asked him what he did, he said he worked in dairy and was impressed by my knowledge. I admitted that everything I knew was because of the Radio 4 docu-drama The Archers and suddenly we were talking about cheese and swapping cheese jokes. They were not good jokes.

Q: what do you call a cheese that isn't

yours?
A: nacho cheese!!!!

Q: what cheese do you use to coax a bear out of a tree?
A: Camembert!!!

Like I say, these were not brilliant jokes but in the moment they had me crying tears of mirth. He was no longer horny, he was too busy laughing. He said that I was a breath of fresh air, that I was the kind of girl he had been waiting all his life for.

Mate, if you have been waiting all your life for a sex worker who is fond of a crap cheese joke then I have to wonder what your life has been like. How would you introduce me to your mother?

"Hi, this is Dee, funny story, I thought her name was Stella for the longest time. Where did we meet? Another funny story actually…"

Not really gonna fly is it? Apart from the fact that, as previously mentioned, I am already married to the man of my dreams, I am not sure that a love of rubbish cheese-based jokes is a firm foundation for a marriage. Though telling me you'd love to take me up the aisle was pretty funny.

Remember when I told you that I was busy introducing men to their own arses? This kind of backfired with Steve. Steve had never even thought about having his arse played with before, thought it was a "bit gay" but I didn't really have any trouble convincing him to do it. He happily did the licking his finger and pretending it was my tongue thing and boy, did he like it. Usually, that is the starting point for me describing a blow job, but I never even got that far with Steve. He started sliding fingers in without being told. When he got to two, I was applauding his dexterity, by the time he got to four, I was starting to suspect that this wasn't in fact his first ride at the anal rodeo.

Bless you Steve and your sobbing with joy as you shot your load, bless you and your rather touching proposal. It was very lovely of you to tell me that if we got married I could finger your arse for you every day, but I am afraid I am going to have to say no.

As I have stated before, I am already married, and hold the fucking phone a minute, who the fuck thinks that my prime function or desire in this life is to give you a daily arse fucking?

I am very happy for you to have discovered (yeah, right, 'discovered') your arse while on the phone with me but how selfish do you have to be to think that I would want nothing of a sexual nature out of a marriage?

Men are selfish on the chat line. Even the ones who say their thing is giving a woman pleasure are only in it for themselves. Don't believe me? Meet Lee who wanted to fulfill my every desire. What I really desired at that moment was a cup of tea and a biscuit, so he was onto a loser from the start really but hey, I was willing to get past that as I only had 40 minutes left to the end of my shift. Forty boring as shite minutes that stretched into an eternity of tedium. I am not joking, I almost fell asleep at one point, I was that fucking bored.

Men, I know you all think of yourself as Mr Blooming Bombastic but really, here is a checklist of what a woman doesn't want. As an aside, I understand that I am painting with broad strokes and though there *may* be women who enjoy the following, I don't know them. #notallwomen #definitelynotthiswoman.

Though she may enjoy having her nipples played with, she does not want you at them forever. Lee described what he was going to do with my nipple for *twenty fucking interminable minutes*. In real life I would have moved him on after five, tops, but on the phone, he was busy telling me it was all for me. Fucksake Lee, if you are going to be describing nipple play then learn to pronounce areola. There is an 'a' at the end of it and every time you said "areole" I wanted to correct you. Wanting to correct someone is not sexy.

Neither, and I am pretty sure I speak for most of us when I say this, are the words 'follicle bumps. "I am running my tongue over your follicle bumps." is not something I wanted to hear, nor is it anything I ever want to hear again. Follicle bumps are not sexy words. You could be Stephen Amell saying them in his gruff Green Arrow voice and it wouldn't be sexy. You could be Josh Homme growling them while his strong arms beat the shit out of his guitar, and it wouldn't be sexy. You could be, fuck it, you get the point. Follicle bumps. Not sexy.

I don't even want to remember the slurpy kissy noises Lee made. "I'm sucking on your nipples now..." *sluuuuuuurp, slurp, slurp slurp, sluuuuuuuurp.* Mate, I have misophonia, I want to stab a body in the neck with a biro if they eat with their mouths open, so it is probably a good thing you were on the end of a phone and not in my presence. You would not have survived. When he wasn't slurping over my follicle bumps, he was so boring that I started to drop off. As a matter of professional pride, and because they can generally tell they don't have your attention if you do, I don't look at my computer or scroll through my phone while I am on a call. If you do that you might mishear something, like the time I heard "I want to step on glass." instead of "I want to slap your ass." I was very confused.

However, Lee was so fucking tedious that I was shopping for books while he did his boring thing and he was so into it, because remember, this was all for my pleasure, that he didn't even notice.

Twenty of the longest minutes of my life later and Lee says the words I really don't want to hear.

"Then I move onto your other breast."

I honestly could have cried. I decided to hatch a plan of escape. It was now five to ten and I was due to come off shift at 10pm. I laid the groundwork.

"I'm sorry honey, you are breaking up a bit, I can't really hear you. No, that's a bit better. Carry on."

I did that three more times and kept it going for longer each time, so he thought there was something wrong with the connection then when it got to 10pm I hung up. I didn't even care about the money for that call, my vagina had got its sewing kit out and was about to declare itself redundant by that point and I had fajitas waiting for me downstairs. Lee, I hope that you just wank next time you call, it would be more honest. You are not doing this all for the woman as you are calling a woman who has no choice but to tell you she is enjoying it. Try that shit on a woman in the real world and see where that gets you. Better still, don't. Talk to women about what they want and do that. That's it. Oh, and never say the words follicle and bump in the same sentence again.

Want to hear about how I killed a man? Who am I kidding? Of course you do. It was the books that reminded me.

I had a regular customer called Pete. I met him on the panty selling site. Older man, really nice and respectful. He liked to listen to me do things. Like play with myself while I watched porn and make a cup of tea. He was a really nice guy and was into the idea of paying for my university reading list. The benevolence (as he saw it) got him off.

Finally, after many calls, he arranged to buy a pair of my knickers. He put a substantial amount of money into my account and then rang me for a session. He was going into hospital for an operation and his daughters were going to take him to theirs so they could nurse him afterwards. The money was to buy the rest of my books. But let's have a good session to see us out. Oh, and would it be ok if he texted me during his convalescence to cheer himself up. Just to see how I was getting on with the Byron. Of course it is Pete. To be honest, I had grown quite fond of him.

At the end of said session, he made quite the strangling noise. I knew I was good, but I didn't know I was *that* good.

And that was the last I heard from Pete. Which was extremely odd. I wasn't expecting to hear from him straight after his operation, but two weeks went past, and I had heard nothing.

So I did some sleuthing. I had his name and address from sending the underwear, so I looked up the obituaries from his area. And there he was. Dead from a heart attack, survived by two daughters, will be sadly missed.

I was devastated. I wrote poems. I laughed like a drain at the idea that the underwear would have arrived on the day of the funeral, and I sent him one last text to say goodbye.

My vagina of doom had claimed her first victim and I didn't know how to deal with it.

Until, 8 months later when I got a text from his number. *Uh oh*, thinks I. The girls have worked out what his security code was, and I am about to get a grilling about who the fuck I am and why I was sending dirty texts to their father. Girding my loins, I opened the text. This is what it said:

"Hello Dee, I hope you are well and you got on ok with the Byron. Sorry I haven't been in touch, been really busy. Love, Pete xxx"

I was not expecting that! After I started to breathe again, I asked him what the fuck had gone on and why there was a fucking

OBITUARY for him. Turns out that he has, or rather, had, a cousin of the same name who also had two daughters and a congenital heart defect who died the day he went into hospital. He wanted to know if we could carry on where we had left off. I pointed out that even though he hadn't died, he had effectively ghosted me.

I know you all have two questions. I shall answer them in turn.

> 1. No, I did not take him back as a client, even though I am very glad he didn't actually die.
> 2. I got on very well with the Byron, thank you.

love, whatever that is

As mentioned before, Stella is the perfect woman. She is like a sex robot made to your specification that has been programmed especially for you with a very dirty laugh and a bawdy sense of humour thrown in for good measure. She is quite the gal.

What she isn't is real.

I'm real. I have real feelings, emotions, hopes and dreams. I have a family, pets, friends and a phobia of snakes. I have a story that is mine and these men who call me cannot have it.

Stella isn't real. Dee is real.

Yet some of them don't get that. The marriage proposals I have had have been (hopefully) tongue in cheek, a way for the man to say thanks for a brilliant orgasm. This is how I have chosen to take them at least because this means I am able to log on the next day.

Sometimes it goes further than I am comfortable with. Remember the guy who wanted me to sob? Paul is creepier. Not because he wants to subject me to anything kinky but because he professes to be in love with me.

Paul is one of the 'it's all for you' brigade of callers. He never ever pleasures himself on the calls and the one time I asked him if he was going to he got really shady and said he had to go.

Paul is a big spender. He takes his time and spends anywhere between half an hour and an hour with me each time.

Paul likes me because I am, in his words, genuine. I am honest with Paul and tell him that I view him as a punter the same as everyone else, but that doesn't deter him, for he thinks that he has made me cum for real. To be fair, so do a lot of the men I talk to, but Paul seems to have taken it to heart.

Paul likes to remember details about what I have said to him before, like the number of cats I have, how tall I am, that blonde isn't my natural hair colour. With someone who I was actually looking to date that would be cute, one of the reasons I fell in love with my husband is that he remembered how I liked my eggs from one time we had breakfast in a hotel together at a conference, five years before we got together, with Paul it feels creepy.

The very first time I allowed Paul to think that he had made me cum was fun. Kept him on the phone for an hour and he felt like a king. It was a close-run thing as to whether I would go into writing or acting, and I sound very convincing on the phone.

To illustrate; when a friend of mine was getting married years ago I was her maid of honour. I had decided, after years of hair fear; it was *very* long at the time, and I hadn't been to a hairdresser for years; that I would brave having a fringe cut in. She knew I was really nervous so arranged for her hairdresser to cut it. When he was done I rang her up with the whole of the staff at the salon trying not to laugh and left a voicemail message sobbing and crying that he had cut it all off and it was a disaster and that I couldn't come to her wedding. It took her two hours to call me back, not because she didn't believe me, but because she did. I think she has forgiven me, I hope she has. Love you Lexi! *blows kisses*

So, back to Paul. He rings me a lot now and there are flags that are being waved to the point where I am seriously considering not taking his calls anymore as it doesn't feel healthy or right. Then again, it is his money, he can spend it as he likes, I still need to eat. It is a real conundrum.

Paul has told me that he is in love with my cunt. That's fine in and of itself but it did feel when he said it like he was testing the waters of saying love. He tells me he wishes he lived nearer then he could come round and see me and take care of me properly. This is one of the reasons I *NEVER* give my actual location. South of England is as specific as I am prepared to get. He has told me that he earns a lot of money and if we were together that I wouldn't have to work on the sex lines, like he is living out a Pretty Woman fantasy where he is Richard

Gere. Though my legs are as long as Julia Roberts' I am not interested in being rescued because I don't need to be. I am doing this job because I want to, not because I have no other choice. I could go and work in a supermarket, not Lidl obviously, fuck Lidl, but I could go out and get work elsewhere. I am doing this job because it suits me to work from home and write chapters in between calls. Enough with your Knight In Shining Armour bullshit.

Paul got edgy and threatened when I told him he wasn't the only customer to make me cum. (Not one of them actually have, I just wanted him to realise that this is my job, and he is not the only one I talk to.) He actually said the words "I feel threatened now" like what we have is special. It really isn't Paul, not at all. The only reason I look forward to you calling is because it means that there is a goodly long time I don't have to be talking to cheap idiots who can't hold off past the information that I have very big tits. You are 12p per minute to me, nothing more.

Paul has now told me that he thinks he is falling in love with me. I was quite stern with him when I told him that of course he was, I was his perfect woman on the phone, that he didn't have to put up with me leaving my teaspoon on the side or farting when I eat falafel. I told him that I did not love him, and I would never love him.

"Maybe one day you will." He said.

Paul worries me sometimes. He works in a solitary job and moved to a new area to do so. He doesn't really know anyone, he doesn't socialize, he has no friends. What he has, in his eyes at least, is a connection to a woman he speaks to for 35p per minute. Ever since I was small, I have had a fascination with serial killers and their psychology, and I recognize a loner with attachment issues when one talks to me. I am very glad that I don't use my real age, name or location because Paul seems to me to be the kind of guy who might track me down out of some misguided idea of love and romance. I worry that if he knew where I was he would turn up. I worry that I would end up another statistic about women who get killed by their stalkers. I worry that even saying that sounds realistic rather than over dramatic.

Paul has not managed to get hold of me for a couple of days as I have been doing different shifts. I am sure that he will get me on the line again at some point, and when he does, then I will gauge what to do about him. I really don't want to say anything that makes him think that our transactions are anything but business to me and I have a feeling that there is something very dark lurking inside him. He scares me a bit. Not for myself, he has no idea who I am, I just hope he never sees another tall blonde with big tits and a dirty laugh and convinces himself that she is me and does something terrible to her.

Because I think that ultimately, Paul thinks of himself as a nice guy, and nice guys scare the shit out of me. They think they are entitled to a woman and that if only the uppity bitches could see what nice guys they were, they would leave the tall alpha males that treated them badly and be with them, the ones who would treat them like queens. The nice guy sees the friendzone as the worst place to be because he places actual friendship with women as lower and not as valuable to his time as a relationship with her. A nice guy sees friendship as second place and the amount of time he puts into it as getting him points towards a sex reward like some kind of grim loyalty card. They think it isn't fair that nice guys like them don't have women. They think that they deserve women because they are nice guys. They make videos about how pissed off they are about it just before they go on a killing spree where the targets are all women.

If you think it is rough that your woman friend thinks of you as a friend, imagine being a woman whose creepy, entitled male friend is only hanging around because he expects sex.

Gods, that was depressing wasn't it? Paul gets to me like that sometimes. Shall we move on to something more frivolous? How about something somewhat surprising?

here come the girls!

When I first started this job I didn't tell many people about it; not because I was embarrassed, I'm not; but because my in-laws are quite old fashioned and I don't think they would get it, hence it isn't splashed all over Facebook. I did tell as select group of people though, they are known as the Stella Fanclub and they have been there all the way through this journey. They are the ones whose group chat I will message at 3am just to tell them about men like Mr Anish Kapoor and they keep me going.

One of them, the one known as Tina Teaspoon, has been asking the same question since day one. She has wanted to know if any women have called.

Finally, I can tell her yes.

Talking to Fran was the answer to a question for me too; namely, would I get turned on with a woman in a way that I knew I wouldn't with a man. The answer was a resounding no. It would seem that sex work for me is work no matter the gender of the caller. It was different, and fun, but I didn't even get a clit twitch.

My male callers have enjoyed hearing about it, that's for sure. There is a real thing among the CIS (not trans) male and heterosexual community where they love to see two women together and I don't get it. I mean I get it from a gay or bisexual woman's perspective, it is hot as fuck, two women, all those boobs, sexy as hell, but not from a straight man's.

Strangely enough though, when my male callers ask me to describe a threesome, unless it involves their wife or girlfriend, it will not be two women they want me to talk about, but me with them and another man. Or two. Or three. In fact, the sky is the limit. I am asked to talk about gangbangs, blowbangs and straight up orgies but not about women together.

It really surprised me as I was fully expecting that my forays into the sapphic would be the thing that turned them on, but whaddya know, the only thing that turns a man on more than his cock is other cock.

    Freud would have a bloody field day if he listened to my calls. He would probably say something about how a man watching a woman getting fucked by multiple cocks is in fact watching a projection of his own fantasy of being fucked by himself many times over.

    Me, I think it is far simpler than that. Men think the world revolves around their cocks, therefore so does the bloody rest of the world. Seriously, watch some gang bang porn. The men on there do not look like they are lucky to be there, more like they are congratulating each other at having cocks. Look at their faces. They're grinning at each other, not at whatever woman is there with them.

    There are also many cuckolds who wish to see their wives fucked by other men. Sometimes it gets them off to think it is me that is giving their other half a good seeing to, but mostly, they want to see her getting another cock. The bigger the better.

Men are strange creatures, and they don't always conform to type. Bless their cottons.

the female of the species is more deadly than the male

Every now and then I hear the words introducing a caller that I dread.

"Group five. Dominatrix."

I am totally shit at being a phone dom. Utterly terrible at it. I cringe when I hear myself because I sound so ridiculous. My callers on this line never last long, not because I am so good, but because I am so bad.

I blame the medium. I am really good at being a dom in real life, spectacular at it. I am a switch so I know how to do things from a sub and dom perspective, but only when I can see what is happening.

"Lick my boots." Doesn't really work well on the phone. I don't know what he is doing, but it won't be licking my boots. Because they are not there. Because we are on the phone.

It all seems rather silly if I am honest and the work ethic kicks in and I feel like I am not giving value for money. I shouldn't give a shit really but for some reason I do. Tonight, I finally gave value for money and made myself feel good at being on the dom line.

I am not going to say this man's name or even make one up. He deserves better than that, I think. He was very much into being humiliated and slapped about. I was quite happy to do that, I quite enjoy getting to vent my patriarchy hating spleen at men now and then, it clears the pipes and makes me smile because I am actually getting paid to do it. I was merrily calling this man a little pussy boy and deriding him for being a virgin at 55 years of age when he tells me that he did once have his face between a woman's legs, but that it was his mother. I was about to terminate the call on the grounds that I don't discuss incest when he starts telling me about her. Jesus shitting Christ she was an abusive piece of shit. This woman would spray his balls with Deep Heat as a punishment then make him perform oral sex on her. And that was just the start of the revelations.

If I was finding the whole thing remotely sexy that would have been the point where I stopped. For a moment I didn't know what to do, I froze. This man was telling me why he was the way he was, why he enjoyed the idea of me slapping him in the face and why he hadn't dared approach a woman sexually in case Mother, who had been dead for fifteen years now, disapproved.

I was fucking horrified.

"She sounds like a right cunt to me." I said before I could stop myself.

"She was my mummy." He whimpered.

I had an idea.

"Call her a cunt."

"I can't."

"I said, call her a cunt."

"I mustn't."

"Who is your mistress?"

"You are Mistress Stella."

"Should you obey your mistress?"

"Yes, Mistress Stella."

"Then call her a fucking cunt."

"She was a cunt."

"Who was?"

"My mother."

"Say it."

"My mother was a cunt."

"Louder."

"My mother was a cunt."

"Louder."

"MY MOTHER WAS A FUCKING CUNT."

When I left him, he was sobbing and saying thank you to me. He was muttering about how he had deserved better and that she was a cunt. I advised him to seek some counselling and he promised me that he would. I hope he does. It would be good to talk to him without the abuse stuff, and 55 isn't that old, he might yet find someone to share his life with. Good luck to you mate, you are going to need it.

Which reminds me of the guy I *hope* I didn't kill.

It had been quite a long call and it was very detailed. He liked to take his time to make sure I was having a good time too (I wasn't but bless him for trying) and was a total gentleman; very respectful in a way that was totally different to Follicle Bump Lee and Creepy Paul. He was a good egg. I hope he still is one, though I can't be sure because a thing happened.

73-year-old men still have needs, I

get that, but if they are going to ring a sex line and talk to Stella, well, there are risks involved. Namely, that she is going to make you cum so hard that you will go quiet, then make strangled noises then repeat "help me" in a weird voice.

I was quite worried about the guy, so I told him to hang up the phone and dial 999 if he needed to. Then I called the office and asked if there was any way they could trace the call I had just taken and see if this guy needed medical attention. They were a bit useless to be honest, said that it was probably just him shooting his load and not to worry. Now, I have had a Transient Ischemic Attack (TIA) or mini stroke at the point of orgasm and it is scary as fuck. I really hope it was just his weird way of having an orgasm, or if it wasn't, that he managed to get some help.

Terry wanted me to actually laugh at his cock. To humiliate him and actually laugh at it. It felt good after all that time of not being able to laugh at my callers to actually let it go. I giggled and laughed and told him that his cock looked like a penis, only smaller and the more I laughed, the more he got off on it and the more that made me laugh.

Then, just to add to the ridiculousness of the whole thing, a daddy long legs flew through the window. I hate those spindly little fuckers with all of my dark heart. There is a childhood trauma I have about them at school which I will probably write a poem about one day and I want them all to die. When my husband is home I dive under my duvet and let him be all manly but when I am on my own, especially if the cats are not in there with me, I have to deal with it.

I dealt with it by chasing it around the bedroom trying to swat it with a cushion, because that was the first thing that had come to hand. Whilst telling Terry that he was unlikely to be able to fuck my arse with that tiny thing, but if I wanted a toothpick I would now know where to find one.

Realising the surreal nature of the situation, I burst out laughing again. Not every day you run round your bedroom, cushion in hand, trying to kill a daddy long legs shouting "Fuck my arse!". At this point I managed to hit the long legged, creepy fucking interloper which fell to the floor only to end up in the mouth of a very happy cat who paraded around for a while with a leg hanging out of her mouth and though it was gross I was happy the shitting thing was dead, so I shouted "YES!". That did for Terry and neither he nor the call lasted much longer.

and now, the end is near

All things it seems, must come to an end. I mentioned about my mental health conditions in earlier chapters and they, along with the sheer amount of work in the second year of university put paid to the Two Stellas.

For me, being a PSO is a summer job. I can do it when I am in a house with lots of people and the sun is out. When my vitamin D levels are higher than my serotonin, I can talk to even the follicle bump guy, but after moving to the Valleys I spend a lot of alone time on my own.

It turns out that this is not ideal for me; I am not good at feeling vulnerable and alone, but I could have kept going if it were not for one thing. The static shifts.

When you sign up you agree to cover either one six-hour or two three-hour shifts. Gods help you if you try to change them too. I can understand that they need to have busy times covered but there is absolutely no flexibility with them, even if all over the summer you have been working pretty much full time for them and are back doing essays and stuff now.

Romanticism and its legacies take precedence over some bloke who wants me to talk him through stretching his arse with a ten-inch dildo and working my shifts always made me hungry for chips, so I took the decision to part ways with this company.

I did ask them if I could come back in the summer when I was not at uni and my mental health was more robust, but they sent me a snotty email saying that they didn't want seasonal workers and that was that.

It did, however, give me more freedom to earn money with the sideline. I had some great reviews and orders were flooding in, so I switched to knickers and videos exclusively. And I am making good money at it. I am also meeting all sorts of people and learning all sorts of things about just how strange a species human beings are.

But that is for another book. For now, from me and all of the Stellas, have fun, don't do anything I wouldn't do and never, ever use your sexy voice to say the words 'follicle bumps.'

At least we will always have Derek.

acknowledgements

Thank you to the Stella Fan Club for keeping me company during the long nights, you bunch of wonderfully weird insomniacs. Thank you also for beta reading and laughing so hard you peed. Me and the Stellas are eternally thankful.

about the author

Dee Dickens Poet and Author likes to make people feel things. Happy, sad, annoyed, it's all the same to her. She lives on a mountain in Wales with her husband and two shedding familiars. She is a UniSlam winner, a poet, author, and masters student at Cardiff Metropolitan University. Dee is queer, black, disabled and woman adjacent. The only thing she isn't is young. And she gives zero fucks about that. She has a chapbook collection out at the moment called The Changeling Child and the Horse and is busy both writing her dissertation and getting her new collection with Whisky & Beards ready. She is a mouthy goddess who cannot be stopped, and she is very, VERY fond of ribs.

Printed in Great Britain
by Amazon